Living into the Answers

Living into the Answers

A Workbook for Personal Spiritual Discernment

Valerie K. Isenhower
and Judith A. Todd

UPPER ROOM BOOKS®
NASHVILLE

The Upper Room® Web site: http://www.upperroom.org

UPPER ROOM®, UPPER ROOM BOOKS® and design logos are trademarks owned by The Upper Room®, A Ministry of GBOD®, Nashville, Tennessee. All rights reserved.

Unless otherwise noted, scripture quotations are from the New Revised Standard Version Bible, copyright 1989, Division of Christian Education of the National Council of the Churches of Christ in the United States of America. Used by permission. All rights reserved.

Scripture noted NIV is taken from the HOLY BIBLE, NEW INTERNATIONAL VERSION® (NIV)®. Copyright 1973, 1978, 1984 by International Bible Society. Used by permission of Zondervan. All rights reserved.

Prayer by Flora Wuellner on page 113 is © 1995 by The Upper Room. Used by permission.
At the time of publication all Web sites referenced in this book were valid. However, due to the fluid nature of the Internet some addresses may have changed or the content may no longer be relevant.

Cover and interior design: Gore Studio, Inc. / www.gorestudio.com
Cover photo: Valerie K. Isenhower
First printing: 2008

ISBN: 978-0-8358-9944-4

LIBRARY OF CONGRESS CATALOGING-IN-PUBLICATION DATA
Isenhower, Valerie K.
  Living into the answers / by Valerie K. Isenhower and Judith A. Todd.
    p. cm.
  Includes bibliographical references and index.
  ISBN 978-0-8358-9944-4 (alk. paper)
  1. Discernment (Christian theology) 2. Spiritual life. I. Todd, Judith A.
II. Title.
  BV4509.5.I83 2008
  248.4—dc222   008001779

Printed in the United States of America

CONTENTS

ACKNOWLEDGMENTS

As the leaders of Water in the Desert Ministries, we have been doing spiritual discernment in our own lives for years and teaching it to others. We wish to thank many people for their contributions to this study of spiritual discernment. These individuals have added to our understanding of the subject. We are grateful to Gordon T. Smith and Thomas Green for their work on personal spiritual discernment, and to Danny Morris, Chuck Olsen, and Ellen Morseth for their contribution to the study of corporate spiritual discernment as it can make a difference in the church today. Spiritual discernment is an ancient practice, and these individuals have contributed to bringing its application forward into our own day. Their books are listed in the bibliography.

We also wish to express our gratitude to those who have read this workbook in its early stages and have offered suggestions and comments to make it clearer and easier to use. We especially thank Elizabeth Thomsen, Diane Taylor, and Gloria Flanery for their careful reading and editorial suggestions. We are encouraged by people who have been willing to field-test the process, especially as they contributed to clarifying how we can approach discernment in our lives.

INTRODUCTION

Personal spiritual discernment is a particular way of facing the issues and decisions of our lives. Because we are people of faith, we learn to place our lives into the context of God's care and keeping. Discernment is a process of listening and choosing based on the understanding that God is to be at the center of decision making. This workbook offers a method of prayerful discernment that many people have found helpful. We pray that this workbook will become a practical tool for deepening your relationship with God.

Before reading any further, stop. Take three deep breaths, then offer the reading and the process of discernment to God. Ask for God's guidance and grace as you begin the journey ahead.

Personal spiritual discernment has been an important part of the faith journey for the leaders of Water in the Desert Ministries. We are committed to practicing discernment in our individual and corporate lives. We understand spiritual discernment to be a major part of the life of mature Christians. Yet the subject is often misunderstood or avoided.

Throughout the workbook we talk about the *movements* of spiritual discernment, because our lives can be compared to a symphony with interconnected movements. Spiritual discernment also is composed of movements, but each one is so deeply connected to the whole that we move in and out of them as themes repeat themselves, and variations arise as new directions are taken. Spiritual discernment is dynamic rather than linear, and the parts flow together rather than proceed strictly from one to another in sequence.

We illustrate the movements of this process as a series of circles. Your personal issue or life question that is the focus for discernment surrounds the process. With God at the center, the content of the circles flows in and out of one another. We provide a visual form for the methodology (page 23). You provide the content.

Using dance as another metaphor for discernment, sometimes the steps follow a pattern, and sometimes they are improvised. In either case, God leads us all into a deeper understanding of our lives and journeys of faith.

Throughout the workbook we will share personal stories. They illustrate the process, and we hope they will trigger similar stories from your own life that help you understand the work of discernment.

Purpose of the Workbook

Discernment helps us discover answers to the questions that arise from issues in our lives. This workbook can be a guide on your spiritual journey. We present the topic of personal spiritual discernment in a practical yet in-depth manner with tools to help you discover God's yearning for your life.

Isolation is actually not the best environment for personal discernment. Note that you can share your journey of discernment with others in several ways. You could use this workbook independently and invite others into the places on your journey where you feel it is appropriate. You could choose to work in a small group with others who are interested in discernment in their own lives. Such a group could gather to discuss each of the movements and how each person is applying them. You could choose to be part of a small group within a corporate spiritual discernment process, using this workbook as a component of the corporate effort.

Look through the whole workbook before you start working with it in depth. You'll get a sense of how the different circles flow. After examining the entire workbook, begin with chapter 1. The first three chapters provide essential foundational pieces for the entire spiritual discernment process. We have observed that when people skip a portion of the workbook, the area omitted will come up and need to be addressed and explored later.

This book is intended to be a *work*book. The activities suggested enable you to progress on your own journey. In each chapter you will find activities, questions for reflection, and space in which to write. In addition to the workbook, you need only a Bible, a pen, and perhaps a journal for any more extensive answers to reflection questions and suggestions. You will find a few blank journaling pages at the end of the workbook to accommodate longer responses to any exercises.

You may also want to repeat portions of the process described in the workbook again and again. As your issues become clearer, your questions will change. As you explore areas of your life more deeply, you will engage in discernment at deeper levels. As God leads you in discernment, you will gain an ability to uncover more of the roots and implications of the issues and discover where God is leading you on your spiritual journey. Thus, repetition of parts of the workbook is both necessary and important.

One purpose for personal spiritual discernment is to get so comfortable with the process that it becomes a part of your life. Each decision becomes an opportunity for living in God's presence more deeply. As Thomas Green says, discernment is the "meeting point of prayer and action."[1] We anticipate that you will find the methodology described in this workbook a helpful way to incorporate spiritual discernment into the decision-making places in your life.

For a church or organization interested in corporate discernment, we recommend using this workbook as a starting point. Small groups formed to use the workbook give members of the corporate body practice in personal discernment before the whole body enters the corporate discernment process.

May you be richly blessed as you explore spiritual discernment and listen for God's purposes for your life.

Living into the Answers

CHAPTER 1

What Is Spiritual Discernment?

DISCERNMENT is a way of sifting priorities and defining a basis for choice. The questions we ask in the midst of the issues that arise in our lives usually center on us and our particular challenges. Personal spiritual discernment shifts the base of our questions. This way of being seeks to listen to God's yearning for us first. This particular process of discernment then places our issues into a larger perspective than just our own lives.

Many people ask us, "How do I know what God wants me to do?" and "How do I know when it is God speaking and not my own voice echoing my desires?" Discernment is the way by which we find the answer to the first question and sort the voices in the second question. Spiritual discernment is about finding God's yearning for the direction of our life. It is not a once-and-for-all answer to our questions but a continual seeking for God's longing as we accept the invitation to live into the abundance God so freely gives us.

As Chuck Olsen has observed, *discernment* is an elusive and mysterious term precisely because it presumes that we can know the will of God.[1] The term *discernment* historically has been used by the Quaker movement and in Roman Catholicism. The Jesuit order has focused time and energy on the discipline of personal discernment. Now the term is becoming an "in" word among mainline Protestants, but people often apply it to anything related to a decision. We will continue to probe the range of its meaning and the rich treasures we can discover as we move within the mystery of God's initiatives and our responses to them.

We do know that spiritual discernment leads to change. Our relationships with God and with other people will never be the same after we begin to live a life of discernment. God may call us to something new in our life. All the time, the Spirit is moving with us, supporting and guiding us.

As individuals we will approach spiritual discernment from a variety of directions because our personality types differ (see chapter 2). We also come to this spiritual activity with varied backgrounds. We are at mixed levels of self-awareness, and we differ in our degree of comfort with our own style of decision making and handling personal issues. We vary also in our relationship with and knowledge of God. Thus, God will speak to us in diverse venues with diverse messages, and we will hear God in just as many ways.

What about that question *How do I know God's will for my life?* We can know God's longing for us more clearly as we become skilled in listening for God and paying attention to the ways God speaks to us. Eventually, as we walk through the process over and over again, discernment becomes a way of life.

We are asked why we don't use the phrase "God's will" in this workbook. In workshops and throughout the book we use the phrase "God's yearning" or "God's longing" instead of "God's will." Often when we speak of God's will, we envision God opening up one path before us, or we look for one answer in the face of our life choices. When we search for God's will in our lives, we can get caught up in looking for "the right answer" or *the* choice God wants us to make. The phrases "God's yearning" or "God's longing" open us up to a larger number of life choices and to a more interactive relationship with the God who calls us into future possibilities. Thus, we have chosen to encourage people to listen to God's longing for us as individual people as we examine issues or decision-making times in our lives.

Discernment is appropriate anytime we have a decision to make. Large or small, the decisions of life point toward particular paths. Paying attention to the process of discerning God's desire starts us on a journey down paths that lead to abundant life.

Pierre Wolff in *Discernment: The Art of Choosing Well* relates spiritual discernment to the following passage from Deuteronomy 30:15-20:

See, I have set before you today life and prosperity, death and adversity. If you obey the commandments of the LORD your God that I am commanding you today, by loving the LORD your God, walking in his ways, and observing his commandments, decrees, and ordinances, then you shall live and become numerous, and the LORD your God will bless you in the land that you are entering to possess. But if your heart turns away and you do not hear, but are led astray to bow down to other gods and serve them, I declare to you today that you shall perish; you shall not live long in the land that you are crossing the Jordan to enter and possess. I call heaven and earth to witness against you today that I have set before you life and death, blessings and curses. Choose life so that you and your descendants may live, loving the LORD your God, obeying him, and holding fast to him; for that means life to you and length of days, so that you may live in the land that the Lord swore to give to your ancestors, to Abraham, to Isaac, and to Jacob.[2]

Because our decisions lead to life or death, discernment involves listening to God, walking in God's way, and choosing life and possibilities. We can see people around us making choices that lead to death, evidenced by divisions between family members and destructive relationships. Choices that bring death lead toward fear and desperation. Life choices bring the opposite results. They foster an opening up of relationships, and these choices lead toward healing and growth. Life choices support the examination of new alternatives in one's life. The Deuteronomist calls us to seek God's longing for our lives, so that we may truly live.

Water in the Desert Ministries began when the four founders discovered that each of us was at a crossroad and transition point in our life. Each of us was facing questions about our life's vocation. After walking through our own personal discernment process, we all met in Albuquerque to discuss the possibilities of a joint venture and to discern whether God was calling us to a special ministry. Our experiences as church leaders helped us to hear people crying out for help with their spiritual hunger. Each of us also has a passion for helping people walk a journey of spiritual formation or renewal. As we looked at the issue of life transitions and prayed for discernment of God's purpose for our meeting, it became clear that God was calling us to provide opportunities for people to grow in their relationship with God. We

For surely I know the plans I have for you, says the LORD, plans for your welfare and not for harm, to give you a future with hope.

—Jeremiah 29:11

found ourselves led to Isaiah 43:18-21, a passage that has become a foundational text for us:

> Do not remember the former things,
>   or consider the things of old.
> I am about to do a new thing;
>   now it springs forth, do you not perceive it?
> I will make a way in the wilderness
>   and rivers in the desert.
> The wild animals will honor me,
>   the jackals and the ostriches;
> for I give water in the wilderness,
>   rivers in the desert,
> to give drink to my chosen people,
>   the people whom I formed for myself
> so that they might declare my praise.

We believe God is doing a "new thing" in our day and longs to bring forth waters in the desert places of people's lives. We have responded to God's yearning by articulating an orderly process for discernment so that others may hear their special call. We each continue personal discernment to find our particular role in the ministry and to explore where God is leading us as a group.

When Is Discernment Inappropriate?

As we enter more deeply into our exploration of God's leading, we can identify the boundaries of the discernment process and look at what discernment is not. Discernment is appropriate when we are seeking to make decisions in the light of God's yearning for us.

However, we also need to know what discernment is not. People often use the term *discernment* to mean "understanding" or "exploration." We can seek to discern our Christian identity through exploration of the Bible and reading various writings about Christian life. We can study the documents, learn the doctrines, and understand the context in which we function as Christians. However, in this workbook "understanding" is not the primary meaning of discernment. Here you will learn to open yourself to God's presence and leading in a more immediate way than is possible through extensive study.

As Gordon Smith reminds us, the process of deciding is not discernment when we confront a choice for which we already know God's commandments. Faced with a choice to commit adultery or to steal something that belongs to another person, we know what path we should choose. We enter into a time of God's leading when we are faced with good decisions, choices, and options. A choice between an evil option and a good option is not discernment. In other words, discernment is not used to test God's commandments. In these cases discernment is not needed because as followers of Christ the decision has already been made.[3]

It is also important to note that discernment is extremely difficult when we find ourselves at the center of an emotional crisis. At such times we cannot hear God's voice with clarity. We need to do some work on the psychological impact of the crisis before we move into discernment. Although we do not need to resolve the crisis completely, we do need to take the time to name what is happening and identify what we are feeling. We will discuss this dynamic further in chapter 4.

It is inappropriate to enter spiritual discernment for another person. The consequences of discerning for someone else are costly. A story illustrates the problem. A woman was very close to her two teenage nieces. The three of them spent a lot of time together, and the woman offered guidance and counseling to her nieces. She began to be concerned about the directions the girls were taking in their lives. She agonized over what she considered inappropriate changes in their lives, and so she began praying. She sought God's desire for the direction her nieces should go and felt she had the answer. One day she sat down and told them what she had discerned for their lives. The girls did not like what she told them. They were furious when she said, "I have been praying for you and have discerned what God wants you to do." Their anger caused the girls to stop talking to their aunt and break off their relationship with her. The aunt thought she had God's answer for them and never expected to be the recipient of their anger over the matter. She discerned for someone other than herself. The loss of the relationship grieved her greatly.

While we cannot discern for another person, we can sometimes receive a word from God for another person, and that word often confirms another's journey. We can pray for guidance as to what to say to someone who wants to talk about their ongoing discernment search. Indeed, it is appropriate to share a word we received from God when asked by the person seeking discernment. We still need to be careful that we do not tell another person what we believe they are to do.

Biblical References to Discernment

Spiritual discernment is not a new process; it is an ancient practice with roots in the biblical text. Most of the stories of discernment in the Bible are partial stories. We do not hear the entirety of the journey the individuals embarked upon. We do find clues to various aspects of discernment. Throughout this workbook biblical references describe processes of prayer and discernment. We invite you to open your Bible and read the passage in context each time you come upon a biblical reference.

The following scripture passages and stories will start us on the biblical journey of discernment:

In Romans 12:1-2, the apostle Paul begins his argument regarding our new life in Christ with the following words:

> I appeal to you therefore, brothers and sisters, by the mercies of God, to present your bodies as a living sacrifice, holy and acceptable to God, which is your spiritual worship. Do not be conformed to this world, but be transformed by the renewing of your minds, so that you may discern what is the will of God—what is good and acceptable and perfect.

The apostle leads us in our journey of faith. He describes a contrast: on one side is becoming *conformed* to the ways of the world. Today these voices of the world call to us through media and common value systems. On the opposite side we are *transformed* through the discernment process in the direction of God's way. The apostle's contrast is instructive for us as we begin to explore what discernment means.

In 1 Kings 19:9-18 Elijah is called to a new understanding of listening to God's voice. No longer will God speak only in earthquake, wind, or fire—all manifestations of power and authority. God will now also speak through the sound of silence, in the still small voice of quiet communication. We cannot hear that small voice easily. We must learn to listen carefully. God's leading may well come at times when we are quiet and attending to the silence in our hearts and minds.

In Acts 9:1-19 we hear about the young man Saul who was persecuting the disciples of Jesus. He believed they were seriously undermining the faith of his fathers. On his way to Damascus, Saul was struck blind and heard Jesus saying to him, "Why do you persecute me?" Saul was thus challenged to enter into discernment, and for three days in his darkness he fasted and prayed. Sometimes we are abruptly called to enter a time of discernment by a question that stops us and forces us to rethink our chosen path and actions.

This story of Saul in Acts includes another discernment section. Already a disciple, Ananias was simply following his daily routine when the Lord appeared to him in a vision and commissioned him to go to a house on Straight Street and to lay his hands on Saul so that he might be healed and regain his sight. It was a clear, straightforward assignment.

However, Ananias protested. He may have said, "Perhaps you haven't heard, Lord, but this Saul is not the kind of person we want to encourage. He's narrow-minded and has the power to destroy us all, and, furthermore, he has some very influential backers who have sent him on this mission of destruction!" In response to the protest, the Lord gave further information that must have astonished Ananias. This person Saul, an opponent of the early church, had a role to play in the future of the church. Ananias trusted the word he received and became God's instrument of healing for Saul.

We too receive the nudging of the Holy Spirit and may even be given tasks to accomplish that seem counterproductive. Ananias helps us see that continuing to listen even when we do not understand is part of our communication with God. New information may even give us a glimpse of the Lord's plans, which are often far larger and more complex than we would even dare to dream.

In the next chapter, Acts 10, Peter receives a call to minister to the Gentiles (outsiders), and in particular, the story focuses on Peter's role in the conversion of Cornelius and his whole household. Peter faces a difficult decision. Outsiders didn't belong and would contaminate the purity of the faith. In a vision, animals considered unclean appear before Peter, and he hears the instructions: "Get up, Peter, kill and eat." Peter also protests, and the vision appears a second and even a third time with the voice adding, "What God has made clean, you must not call profane." Peter listens to God, and his understanding of insiders and outsiders is stretched. The outcome is a radical shift to baptizing Gentiles into the Christian faith.

The Process of Discernment

Our present use of the English word *discernment* comes from the Latin root, which means to separate, to distinguish accurately one object from another. The content of the word *discernment* comes from the two Greek verbs: *dokimazo,* meaning to regard something as worthwhile or appropriate, to discover, or to prove, and *diakrino,* which means to distinguish, separate, prefer, or to judge one thing to be better than something else. Both Greek verbs are translated "to discern" with the implication of testing or judging. In the process we describe in this workbook, *discernment* allows a person to see clearly and to distinguish between alternatives. The process moves us into choices and discriminates among alternatives.

When people hear the word *process,* many think of a list of tasks or activities to be completed in order to arrive at a desired outcome. When we refer to *process,* we are talking about a movement through the way of discernment that is neither linear nor a checklist of items to be completed. Spiritual discernment opens up a way to find new solutions offered to us by God at points where old ways won't work anymore. The old ways are what we are doing now, and the solution is where God is leading us. We must be willing to walk through a process of change.

In order to live the life God yearns for us to have, we must let go of where we are now and what we love in order to live into the bigger place to which God is calling us. We have to be willing to endure chaos and not know where it will all end in order to experience new life. The story of Creation in Genesis is a prime example of order coming out of chaos.

Chaos will reign in the middle of the discernment process, but we must be willing to go there. As the process begins and you open yourself to change, ask God to put you back together as you come out of the chaos, understanding that

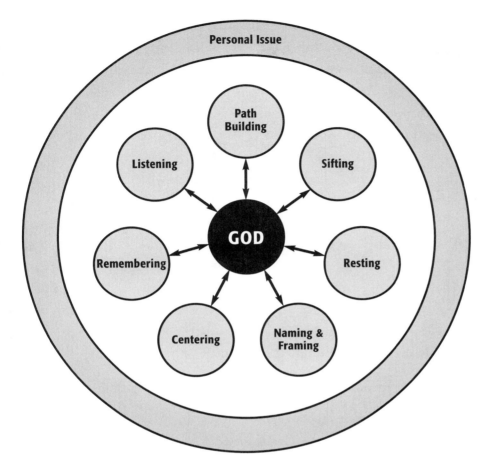

The Movements in Discernment

you will not emerge the same. Expect the process of moving through chaos to creation and new solutions to lead to a life that is bigger, deeper, and richer.

The process of spiritual discernment with movement from chaos to new creation is not about techniques. Mastering techniques is not the route to being proficient in spiritual discernment. Spiritual discernment is an art. It takes time and patience.

Most people can learn the techniques of any art form, but unless one has an eye for the "picture," something is missing. Val is a landscape photographer. She takes photographs while the rest of us take pictures because she has an eye for the balance and focus of the finished product. Discernment is an art too because we train our eye to look toward God's yearning. Accordingly we need to take the time to educate our spirit to walk through the process. Keep in mind that the process of discernment is not linear; it is not like steps on a ladder. Although we tend to want our lives to keep getting better and better, and we wish to progress from where we are into the future along a straight line, life isn't like that. We need to realize that the discernment process is cyclical and takes time.

Our image for the discernment process, shown on page 23, consists of a series of circles connected in the center by God. A large circle surrounds the series of circles, representing the issue or decision we are focused on. Holy indifference fills the spaces between the circles (see chapter 5).

We begin the process by asking for God's leading as we work with our issue or choice and then move into the various circles. We move back and forth from circle to circle. In order for the process to be complete, we need to enter each circle. When we try to skip a circle, we will find that we keep returning to it. The image is designed in a circular fashion because often we will keep coming back to the same spot, each time going a little deeper and letting go of what binds us at one level only to return to the issue at a new level.

Resting During the Journey of Discernment

As we walk through the process of discernment, we uncover information, read, look at our lives, and listen for God's voice. These activities stir up the water of wisdom and understanding around us. Wayne Muller quotes the Tao Te Ching, "Who is it that can make muddy water clear? But if allowed to remain still, it will gradually become clear of itself." Wayne calls this "spiritual gravity." Rest allows the water of our work to settle and for the results of our work to find their places. When we push on through without stopping, our discernment process becomes counterproductive. Resting allows for clarity and the quiet that gives us wisdom.[4]

Resting offers space for that which we have heard in our mind and felt in our heart to catch up with God. These thoughts and feelings will continue to muddy the waters if we don't stop to rest in God. It is God—not our activity—that makes the water clear. Resting is listening in a different way. Resting through-out the process helps make our vision a little clearer.

Rest is a way of saying we are not in control. It is an avenue for bringing balance into the process. Rest reminds us to let go and remember that we are seeking God's yearning and not what we can accomplish or make happen. We talk more about rest in chapter 10. We suggest you read that chapter before starting your discernment process. In the meantime, here are some suggestions to help you rest along the way:

- Learn your own rhythms of work and rest. Individuals who push through to completion before stopping to rest will need to be deliberate about their decisions to rest between each circle of the discernment process. While rest is essential, it does not substitute for the work of discernment. Look for balance between work and rest throughout the process.

- Once a week stop and be present with God and God alone. During this time lift up the process and give it to God. Then relax and enjoy God's presence and the renewal of the Spirit without wondering what comes next or what God is trying to say to you.

- When you feel overwhelmed or stuck, walk away for a while. The harder we try the harder it is to hear. Put this workbook aside and stop thinking and praying about the process. Go on a sabbath walk. Wayne Muller describes a sabbath walk as a time without purpose and space without need for revelation. Take thirty minutes to walk slowly, letting your senses be your guide. If something catches your eye, stop and linger, allowing the moment to be. When it feels right, move on along your walk. There is no need to hurry. When you are called to stop, stop. When you are called to move, move. At the end of thirty minutes observe how you feel physically, emotionally, and spiritually. Write these thoughts down, and pick up the workbook again when resting has renewed your soul.

Looking for Certainty in the Process

Before we move into the next chapter and begin our journey, we need to discuss one last subject. Many people say to us, "I have gone through discernment, but how can I know for sure that I have heard God correctly?" We can't be sure! However, we can have some confidence in the midst of the journey. Gordon Smith reminds us of 1 Corinthians 13:12: "For now we see in a mirror, dimly, but then we will see face to face. Now I know only in part; then I will know fully, even as I have been fully known." We may not have certainty in this life, but if we continue to be honest, to be faithful, and to trust in God, we can live in confidence that God will honor our work.[5] Thomas Green puts it this way: God does not ask us be right, but God does ask us to be honest in our discernment work.[6]

CHAPTER 2

Presuppositions

ALL OF US enter discernment with a set of assumptions about life and about God. We base these assumptions on our experiences and what we have been taught. These assumptions become the presuppositions we use when seeking discernment, the personal foundations from which we start the way of discernment.

When we set about the journey to discern God's yearning for our lives, we must explore these presuppositions. Recognizing and acknowledging the foundation on which we base our decisions begins to open us up to what God wants. In this chapter we will examine the following foundational pieces:

- our own personality type and decision-making processes
- our images for God
- our assumptions about how God interacts with us
- our own inner life.

Personality Types

Our own personalities affect the way we make decisions. Strengths and weaknesses characterize each personality type. Knowing what they are allows us to be aware of them during the discernment process.

Many people are familiar with the Myers-Briggs personality types. The questions and types developed by Isabel Briggs Myers and Katharine Cook Briggs are now widely used in church circles and across denominations. Each of us operates mainly out of one perspective in each of the four pairs of preferences. The summary descriptions that follow serve as reminders for those familiar with the types.

If the Myers-Briggs Types are new to you, you can explore the types online at www.personalitypathways.com/type_inventory.html. When you search online for "Myers-Briggs Types," you will discover many Web sites. A simplified version, the Keirsey Temperament Sorter, is available in a book by David Keirsey and Marilyn Bates, *Please Understand Me: Character and Temperament Types*.[1]

> **Extrovert / Introvert:** An extrovert processes data externally, while an introvert will process the same data internally.
>
> **Sensing / Intuitive:** A sensate deals mainly with the actual and the factual and usually needs to experience something in order for it to be real. An intuitive person is more interested in future possibilities and tends to have hunches as to what comes next.
>
> **Thinking / Feeling:** A thinking type person is rational, logical, generally ruled by the head rather than the heart, and tends to make decisions based on objective data. The feeling person is aware of others' feelings, makes decisions based on personal values and the likes and dislikes of others. The feeling person generally is ruled by the heart rather than the head.
>
> **Judging / Perceiving:** The judging person wants matters settled, is decisive, and lives a planned, orderly life. A perceiving type tends to be flexible, is always looking for more data and so is reluctant to make a decision.

Knowing where we fit in each category gives us a clue about where we will have difficulty and where we will be at ease in discerning God's longing for us. For more information on Myers-Briggs Types, see Chester P. Michael and Marie C. Norrisey, *Prayer and Temperament: Different Prayer Forms for Different Personality Types* or Keirsey and Bates, *Please Understand Me*.

Other personality inventories, such as the Enneagram, can be fruitful when exploring your foundational assumptions. The Enneagram, based on nine fundamental personality types and their complex relationships, is rooted in spiritual wisdom and can be adapted by most religious traditions. For more information on the Enneagram, see *The Wisdom of the Enneagram* by Don Riso and Russ Hudson. You can take a self-scoring Enneagram test on their Web site: www.enneagraminstitute.com. *The Enneagram and Prayer*, by Barbara

Metz and John Burchill, offers additional information on the types and prayer.

The strengths and weaknesses of each personality category affect the way individuals handle the discernment process. For example, the sensing person will want all the facts and will have a more difficult time in the path-building circle (chapter 8). The intuitive person will tend to leap ahead and may miss some important pieces. The thinking person's tendency to rely on logic can result in some difficulty listening for the stirrings of the Holy Spirit. The feeling person may be challenged in separating his or her interior feelings from the voices of other people. Finally, the perceiving person will have a hard time bringing the process to a close because there always may be one more possibility to explore.

Knowing your own personality type and tendencies makes moving through the discernment circles clearer. The more information you have about how you work with information and feelings, the better you will handle the complexities of the journey into discernment.

Images for God

Another set of presuppositions we bring to discernment centers on our images for God. We have been taught to "see" God in particular ways, especially if we have grown up in the church. We may have shifted some of those images as we have walked our faith journey. On the other hand, we may still work from a primary image for God learned as a child. The way we understand who God is affects our faith development and our view of our relationship with the Trinity. Depending upon how we understand God to interact with us, we will trust the process of discernment and its outcomes as led by God, or we will have difficulties with it.

What are your images for God? If you are a visual learner, you may be able to visualize and perhaps even draw your image or images for God. However, we have found that American mainline Protestants tend to experience God as a feeling (such as love or warmth) rather than an image (such as shepherd or fortress). If you are an auditory learner, you may sense God through music or in the sounds of nature. If you are a tactile learner, you may understand God's presence through lighted candles or incense or through items you can touch, like a cross. People experience God in a variety of ways, and no one way is the "right" way.

The Bible presents multiple images for God through the written word. We may feel more comfortable with some images than others. Because the Hebrew people understood that God could not be contained in any one representation, they employed various images so that no single one would be primary. Although Jesus calls God "Father," and we have adopted that language as dominant, other views of God appear in the New Testament as well.

Many of us developed assumptions about the ways God comes to us from Sunday school materials and pictures of Jesus on the walls of church corridors. Our images often are grounded in biblical passages such as Isaiah 6 where God sits on the kingly throne, high and lifted up, shrouded with the mystery of incense smoke and surrounded by the seraphim.

We may see God seated in the throne room described in Revelation 4 or Ezekiel 1:26-28. These images have become familiar through the hymns and music of the church. Many can envision the throne scene of Revelation 4 as expressed in the hymn written by Reginald Heber in 1826, "Holy, Holy, Holy! Lord God Almighty," especially stanza 2:

> Holy, holy, holy! All the saints adore thee,
> casting down their golden crowns around the glassy sea;
> cherubim and seraphim falling down before thee,
> which wert, and art, and evermore shalt be.

Or perhaps Daniel 7:9-10 describes your primary image for God: the Ancient of Days, seated on the throne, hair as white as snow, presiding over the court that sits in judgment. This English hymn from 1757 interprets the images from Daniel 7:

> Come, thou almighty King,
> help us thy name to sing,
> help us to praise!
> Father, all glorious, O'er all victorious,
> come and reign over us, Ancient of Days!

We find the almighty-king image—transcendent, ruling over all things, and worthy of praise—strongly represented in the hymnody and liturgy of the Protestant church, especially prior to the 1950s.

Jesus is also presented through song and scripture as the transcendent one, worthy of our praise and worship (Rev. 5:11-12), a high priest who effects our salvation (Heb. 7:23-28). Before this figure all shall bow the knee and confess Jesus as Lord (Phil. 2:10-11). The transcendent imagery separates us from the Christ as unworthy humans who are in relationship by grace alone and subject to judgment as we make decisions and live our lives.

On the other end of the imagery continuum are the intimate, personal, and anthropomorphic images for God. We find both transcendent and immanent images for God in the first two chapters of Genesis. Creator of all, the powerful God speaks the world into being and calls it good in Genesis 1. Yet, in Genesis 2:7, we see God forming the human being (*'adam*) from the earth (*'adamah*) and breathing the breath of life into each nostril. The intimate and tender portrait of Genesis 2 balances the powerful and omnipotent imagery in Genesis 1, and we are brought to a broader understanding of our God through both chapters. We are not asked to choose between the portraits. We are asked to hold both ends of the continuum as essential to our conceptualization of the God with whom we are in relationship.

In the same way, Jesus is the incarnate God who shares our humanity and knows what it is to be tempted as we are. Born human and raised in an extended family, Jesus begins his ministry by spending time in the Judean wilderness and being tempted there (Matt. 4:1-11; Mark 1:12-13; Luke 4:1-13). His touch heals (Mark 1:31, 5:41; Luke 13:13); his words set people free (Mark 5:13; Luke 7:48-50; Matt. 6:25-33); and he is seen with outcasts and sinners (Mark 2:15-17; Luke 19:1-10; Matt. 11:16-19). The early Christian hymn in Paul's letter to the church in Philippi explains the both/and nature of our Lord in this way:

> Let the same mind be in you that was in Christ Jesus,
> who, though he was in the form of God,
>> did not regard equality with God as something to be exploited,
> but emptied himself,
>> taking the form of a slave,

> being born in human likeness.
> And being found in human form,
>   he humbled himself
> and became obedient to the point of death—
>   even death on a cross.—PHILIPPIANS 2:5-8

Both transcendent and immanent images give us ways to connect with the God who loves us and who wants to be in relationship with us. We are created in God's image. Our humanity and all creation reflect the many ways we experience God's activities.

> Then God said:
> "Let us make humankind ['adam] in our image, according to our likeness; and let them have dominion over the fish of the sea, and over the birds of the air, and over the cattle, and over all the wild animals of the earth, and over every creeping thing that creeps upon the earth."
> So God created humankind ['adam] in his image,
>   in the image of God he created them;
>   male and female he created them.
> God blessed them, and God said to them, "Be fruitful and multiply, and fill the earth and subdue it; and have dominion over the fish of the sea and over the birds of the air and over every living thing that moves upon the earth.—GENESIS 1:26-28

We may have explored the Bible enough to be able to see and incorporate the masculine, the feminine, and even the gender-neutral images for God we find in the biblical text. The masculine images for God as shepherd (Ps. 23; Isa. 40:11), as mighty warrior (Exod. 15:1-3; Ps. 68), or as a potter (Isa. 64:8) highlight particular aspects of God's relationship with us. Feminine images for God as mother (Isa. 42:14; 49:13-15; 66:7-13), as midwife (Ps. 22:9-11), or as a seamstress (Gen. 3:21; Luke 12:27-28) call up a different set of relational connections. Even God understood as a rock (Ps. 71:3), refuge (2 Sam. 22:2-4), or mother eagle (Deut. 32:11-12) evoke unique aspects of the multifaceted relationship between God and humans. The many images for God give expression to the many ways God comes to us at different times in our lives.

Some "images" are more feelings than they are visuals, for instance, sensing God as spirit breathing or plucking our heartstrings when we are deeply moved are additional ways to sense God's presence. Feeling the solidness of the rock of God's protection, the protectiveness of a new mother with her infant, or the powerfulness of a mighty ruler add dimension and range to our perceptions of God's presence. All our senses can be a part of experiencing God in our lives.

Along with looking at our images for God, we need to understand ourselves to be in relationship with the triune God. When we explore how we relate to God, to Jesus, and to the Holy Spirit, we can begin to know how the Trinity interacts with us in relationship and what we believe is expected of us. As we examine the biblical imagery for God, we will expand our vision of the One who is bigger than we can imagine and who is active in our lives.

The following series of exercises will help you discover how you view your relationship with the triune God and explore biblical images for God that may be unfamiliar. Work through the exercises and return to them often.

Before you do the exercises, you may want to identify your primary image for God and some characteristics of God with which you feel comfortable. Following the exercises, consider how your images for God may have changed and how these changes affect you.

When I pray, I imagine God as: (Describe or draw your image.)

I am comfortable/uncomfortable with many images for God because:

How have my images for God changed during my lifetime?

How do I experience God/Jesus/the Holy Spirit now?

How would I describe the ways God/Jesus/the Holy Spirit relates to me?

The following exercise lists biblical verses that contain a variety of images for God. As you look up each set of verses, identify the image, and then find the verbs or characteristics the image represents. These images for God enable us to see how God was visualized within the biblical texts. This exercise encourages you to explore the Bible for yourself.

Biblical Images for God

Look at the following biblical passages and write down the images for God

Scripture	God is like: (description)	God's activities: (verbs)
2 Samuel 22:2-4	a rock, fortress	one who delivers, saves
Psalm 123:2		
Isaiah 64:8		
Genesis 3:21		
Hosea 13:7-8		
Luke 12:27-28		
Luke 13:34		

Scripture	God is like: (description)	God's activities: (verbs)
Job 10:8-12		
Deuteronomy 32:11-12		
John 3:3-7		

How do these images affect your ability to trust God?

What new images might help you as you enter a process of spiritual discernment?

The next exercise helps you identify some ways you have already experienced God in your life.

Experiencing God

As you consider your images for God, recall ways you have experienced God in your lifetime. List about ten adjectives that describe God (such as eternal, kind, powerful, loving, judging, distant, personal, etc).

Now choose three of the adjectives and write a paragraph for each that describes times when your experience of God matches that adjective. For example, if you chose loving, distant, and powerful, start by writing about an experience of a loving God that you remember. Do the same for the other two words.

Now, remember what you were taught about God as a child. How does that teaching match or differ from your own experiences of God?

Ask another person to do this exercise. Then share your list and experiences with that person, listening for similarities and differences. Talk about how you each understand the ways God has been involved in your life.

Finally, note how your relationship with God has changed with the different experiences. Recall any biblical images for God that match your own experiences.

In the next exercise you identify how you sense God in different settings.

Finish each sentence describing how you sense God in that situation.

1. When I have experienced a loss, I sense God . . .

2. When my back is against the wall, I sense God . . .

3. When I see a rainbow, I sense God . . .

4. When I make a mistake, I sense God . . .

5. When I am quiet, I sense God . . .

6. When something unexpected happens, I sense God . . .

7. When I hear a special piece of music, I sense God . . .

Look over your sentences, and notice anything that surprises you. Has your understanding of God (or yourself) changed as you have completed the three exercises?

As we open up and explore our assumptions about the ways God comes to us, we will become aware of the strengths and limitations we place upon God's interactions with us. Wilke and Noreen Cannon Au have described the psychology of the power of the images for God. How we perceive God influences how we see ourselves and how we live our lives. Our images for God are critical to our religious experience because we meet God as the one we image God to be.[2] We need to continue to examine our assumptions as they arise within the discernment process.

Assumptions About God's Interaction with Us

After exploring our images for God and recognizing the ones that rise to the surface for us, we can go on to name some of our assumptions about how God relates to us as humans.

Danny E. Morris and Charles M. Olsen name three important assumptions:[3]

"She would have been a different person, if she had had a different God," lamented a woman about her recently deceased friend who lived a God-fearing, though severely repressed and unhappy, life.

—The Discerning Heart

1. "We assume that God is self-disclosing and that God yearns for the created world and enters into a covenant relationship with God's people."

   The God whom we worship is connected to the human community and cares about us deeply. The Bible witnesses again and again to the ways God yearns to be in relationship. Exodus 19 and Hosea 1–4 both show the covenant relationship and God's yearning for relationship with us.

2. "We assume that God enters into human existence with such vulnerability that people . . . are drawn into the vulnerability of God."
   The early Christian hymn in Philippians 2 declares the vulnerability with which Christ came into the world.

> Let the same mind be in you that was in Christ Jesus,
> who, though he was in the form of God,
> did not regard equality with God
> as something to be exploited,
> but emptied himself,
> taking the form of a slave,
> being born in human likeness.
> And being found in human form,
> he humbled himself
> and became obedient to the point of death—
> even death on a cross.—PHILIPPIANS 2:5-8

3. "We assume that the indwelling Holy Spirit is the active and ongoing guide in personal and corporate discernment."
   Jesus tells us in John 14 that when he is gone, God will send the Holy Spirit (the Advocate, Counselor, and Helper).

And I will ask the Father, and he will give you another Advocate [Guide], to be with you forever. . . . You know him, because he abides with you, and he will be in you.

But the Advocate, the Holy Spirit [Guide], whom the Father will send in my name, will teach you everything, and remind you of all that I have said to you.—JOHN 14:16-17, 26

In order to trust the discernment process, we have to assume that God is willing and eager to share God's longing with us. If we do not believe God wants to disclose this information and guide us through the Holy Spirit into finding God's yearning, then it is difficult to walk the journey of discernment.

What assumptions do I have about how God relates to humanity in general? What do I assume about God's relationship to me in particular?

How are these assumptions helpful or not useful to the process?

Where do I need to examine my assumptions in order to hear God's desire for me and my life of abundance and blessings?

Jesus' baptism is a paradigm story that further shapes how we understand our relationship with God and how that relationship affects spiritual discernment. Author Wendy Wright describes a sermon she heard on Jesus' baptism and his time in the wilderness, a time in which he had to discern the spirits. The preacher repeated the words Jesus heard at his baptism: "This is my Son, the Beloved, with whom I am well pleased" (Matt. 3:17). The preacher went on to emphasize that before Jesus entered the wilderness and a time of discernment, he was claimed as a child of God and told he was loved. We find it beneficial to understand our identity as children of God and to know God loves us before we begin the journey of discernment.[4]

How do I know God loves me?

If I accept the assumption that God loves me, how do I feel?

How do I see myself as a child of God?

Repeat the following sentence often so that you internalize this understanding.

"This is my son/daughter _____ , my beloved, with
(your name)
whom I am well pleased!"

We tend to pray about our problems, concerns, and needs, and forget that God wants to participate in other areas of our lives. Just as we enjoy being part of the lives of family and friends, God longs to be included in the totality of our lives. A story from Judith illustrates her new appreciation for God's involvement in all of life:

> I recall when I was a young adult in the midst of the decision-making process about buying a new car. I had found one I liked, and it was one of the last two the dealer had from the previous year. The choice was between a lime green or a butterscotch orange, and the dealer was offering a good price on either car. The car was a Fiat, and I was receiving advice from several sources that Fiats were unreliable cars. I was stuck in the midst of my decision making, when I called home to receive parental advice. The advice my father gave me stopped me in my tracks. He said, "Have you taken your dilemma to God?" I must admit it had never occurred to me that God would be interested in whether or not I bought this particular car. I grew a lot in my spiritual understanding with that question. God does care! I did learn to open up my decision making in order to let God in. I bought the car and enjoyed driving

my "Butterscotch Drop" for many years. And I learned that allowing God to become a major player in such decisions not only makes the decisions easier but also adds another strand to the deepening spiritual relationship.

Exploring the Inward Life

As we begin to identify our images for God and name the complexities of our relationship with God, we also will begin exploring our inward life. In our day this exploration is a difficult journey. Most people have not been taught the spiritual disciplines (see chapter 3), nor have they learned to speak about the feelings that grow out of the yearnings of our hearts. Instruction about how to pray, meditate, and open ourselves to God is no longer part of the training we receive in church or at home. And sometimes we have covered over our feelings to such an extent that we do not know how we feel or how to sort our deepest emotions.

First, a word of warning: listening and paying attention to God's yearning for us may well lead us into the wilderness. As we examine a particular issue and ask the questions that enable us to address it, God may show us that the real issue is not what we initially framed. We may, indeed, discover prior issues that affect our current focus. Perhaps God will lead us into the wilderness of a deeper issue we may not wish to address.

Wilderness time can be positive. As we experience the journey, we can learn to depend upon God alone to lead us through the desert-like places. The wilderness time also can be a challenge, for it may be a time of testing and trial. Usually the experiences in the wilderness and the experiences of God's leading are both positive and challenging at the same time.

The biblical passages about Jesus in the wilderness give us the paradigms for placing our own journeys into perspective. Our ongoing relationship with God includes continual reminders of our identity as children of God and of God's love for us. Exercises like *lectio divina* (see chapter 3) help us internalize these messages from God.

Thus, the work of spiritual discernment may take us into places where we confront the unexamined portions in our lives and the challenge of our greatest fears. These confrontations can be hard work. A counselor or spiritual director can be a big help as we walk into the struggle-places of our own lives.

Working with a person trained in psychological processes or in spiritual direction provides perspective and insight into our process of discovery. Needing to reach out to another person for reflection upon our discoveries is a natural part of discernment. We may want to be alert to the people God places along our path to walk with us.

Of course it is important to align ourselves with Christ, the "author and perfecter of our faith" (Heb. 12:2, NIV). Our faith in Christ keeps us centered over the course of discernment. It is Jesus' baptism and wilderness struggle that give us hope and remind us of God's love. It is through Jesus that we receive the gift of the Holy Spirit to guide us. It is through Jesus that we receive the grace needed to walk the journey of discernment. Finally, our allegiance to Christ is the centering point from which we operate; it keeps our eyes focused on God's longing and not the desires of our own hearts.

The spiritual disciplines and prayer undergird the work of discernment and the inward journey. Both can be effective individually and in community. The support of others along the way enables us to listen more clearly to God's voice speaking to us through the disciplines. Even though this workbook addresses the personal pilgrimage, these journeys cannot be taken in isolation from communities of faith. We often develop small groups of people who are interested in journeying with us. These communities of faithful people give depth, dimension, and perspective to our individual journey.

CHAPTER 3

Personal Spiritual Practices

AS WE LEARNED in chapter 1, discernment requires us to pay attention to God's leading, and it involves intense and intentional listening. In this chapter we will look at Christian spiritual practices that can enhance our journey of discovery by improving our listening skills.

One cannot engage in spiritual discernment without an ongoing relationship with God. God yearns to be in deeper relationship with us and seeks avenues to touch us. By focusing on our images for God, we have begun to identify the nuances of our relationship. Learning new images for God and discovering new ways God is present in our lives leads to a more multifaceted relationship.

In any relationship, the more we know about the other person, the more we can understand that person's ways of approaching the world. The same is true in our relationship with God. God's yearning for our lives continues to emerge as the relationship develops. When we pay attention to reading the Bible and to prayer—the building blocks of that relationship—we will be able to listen as God speaks to us and calls us into wholeness. Discernment, according to Thomas Green, "can normally be only as deep and as solid as that relationship itself. The true discerner must be a praying, loving person."[1]

The Spiritual Disciplines

Spiritual disciplines are tools to use in deepening our relationship with the triune God. Dallas Willard in *The Spirit of the Disciplines* understands the disciplines as a way to align with Christ by participating in the activities Jesus practiced. These activities include prayer, solitude, study, and meditation upon God's Word.[2] The disciplines arise out of our "longing after God."[3]

You can find the spiritual disciplines that fit you best by exploring a variety of them. Some of these practices will come more naturally than others. Each can be learned and will, with practice, become easier. Choose to focus on the ones where you are most comfortable.

There are many spiritual disciplines, and we encourage you to read more about them in the books available on the subject, including those by Richard Foster, Dallas Willard, and Daniel Wolpert. A list of disciplines varies depending on the source you read. The following list, along with basic descriptions, covers the major disciplines:

- **Prayer**–practiced in many forms, prayer is our soul's conversation with God;

- **Meditation**–focusing on a word, phrase, or concept from the biblical text, meditation is a way to hear God's voice in our life;

- **Contemplative Silence**–clearing our mind allows God to speak to us from the depths of our soul;

- **Study**–reading the Bible deepens our understanding of the triune God and teaches about the ways we should live our lives;

- **Sabbath Keeping**–setting a day aside helps us reconnect with our Creator;

- **Worship**–giving glory to God in the midst of the Christian community;

- **Hospitality**–showing God's love for all by allowing our relationship with God to flow out of us and into the lives of others;

- **Spiritual Friendships**–connecting with those Christians around us who keep us spiritually grounded in the faith;

- **Works of Compassion**–working toward peace and justice in this world.

Prayer

Prayer is conversation with God that takes place through word and silence. We tend to talk to God, but we also need to go into the silence, to dive into the deep inner space of prayer and contemplation. Discovery and exploration of prayer types and styles enhance our understanding of this discipline's breadth and potential.

Each of us is drawn to different types of prayer. No one method of prayer is the "right way" for everyone. Our personality type can be a determining factor in what works most effectively. The book *Prayer and Temperament* by Chester Michael and Marie Norrissey suggests various styles of prayer to fit the various personality types. Another indicator is the activities we enjoy. In her book *A Praying Congregation*, Jane Vennard says we can discover how we pray by becoming attentive to what we do to renew our spirits and to nurture our souls.[4] She describes the ways these activities can become the means to practice the presence of God.

One style of prayer that most people find fruitful is called *lectio divina,* or sacred reading. It incorporates different prayer types in the process of praying the scripture. But before we explain *lectio divina,* we need to talk about preparing ourselves to listen to God.

Listening

The internal conversation going on inside our head makes it difficult to listen to God. Our challenge is to quiet those thoughts so that God's still small voice can be heard. John Ackerman in *Spiritual Awakening,* says, "Listening to God may be like listening to another person at a noisy party. Other people may interrupt."[5] The background noise sometimes interrupts the main conversation, and our attention shifts away from God.

We are so full of all the details of our lives, worries, anticipation of events ahead of us, and struggles with past events that it is not easy to focus and open up the space to allow ourselves to listen. Judith has appreciated a poem by Sir Thomas Browne quoted by Madeleine L'Engle in her book *A Ring of Endless Light*. The poem, which happens to use a masculine image of God, expresses God's response to our lack of space inside for listening to God.

> If thou could'st empty all thyself of self,
>   Like to a shell dishabited,

Then might He find thee on the ocean shelf,
        And say, "This is not dead,"
And fill thee with Himself instead.

But thou art all replete with very thou
        And hast such shrewd activity,
That when He comes He says, "This is enow
        Unto itself—'twere better let it be,
It is so small and full, there is no room for me."[6]

We can learn how to silence the noise of all that goes on around us as we focus our thoughts on God in prayer. This process of providing space for God to speak so that we may hear is ongoing. Although we can hear God speaking to us through the experiences of our everyday lives, we listen most easily when we are attentive and relaxed and in a quiet atmosphere. Here is an exercise that introduces you to contemplation, a quiet way of opening yourself up and listening to God.

> Being silent before God is not easy and does take practice. Find a quiet place that feels peaceful. Sit comfortably and relax. Set a time of five or ten minutes at the beginning, gradually lengthening the time to twenty minutes. Begin by learning to be present to your surroundings using a phrase such as "I am present to . . ." my chair, the tree outside my window, my pet in the room with me, the sound of birds, traffic, or the wind. Next pay attention to your breathing and relax into its rhythm. Finally, repeat to yourself, "I am present to my God" as you open up to God's presence. Repeat the phrase when your mind begins to wander and you need to refocus on God. You may want to write in a journal about your experience.

Lectio Divina

We are often so full of questions and uncertainties that God's voice can't get through the chatter. We can create the space inside our mind and heart for God's presence in another way through reading and meditating on the Word of God. The challenge is to read the Bible attentively and slowly, in a manner that highlights the details in the text. Read in this way, the Bible becomes an opening to hear more clearly what God is saying to us.

Lectio divina is such a way to read the Bible, one practiced in the Roman Catholic church for centuries. Assuming that God continually reaches out to us to be in relationship with us, we need a process for listening. This method of listening involves hearing a portion of the scripture read repeatedly. In *lectio divina* the rhythm of the listening is made up of a series of movements into and out of the biblical text. The prayer has four parts, each represented by a Latin word.

Lectio	reading, paying attention
Meditatio	thinking about the passage, letting it sink into feeling, into the heart
Oratio	praying simply and briefly
Contemplatio	being with God in the silence

Pick a portion of scripture, preferably a story. No one scripture passage works for everyone. The process works best if various passages are used over time. If you aren't sure which scripture to use, refer to the Revised Common Lectionary for the week's designated passages.

Find a comfortable place to sit and relax in silence.

Lectio:	Read the scripture aloud and notice what word or phrase strikes you. Read it again and see whether your mind stays on the same word or phrase.
Meditatio:	Think about the word or phrase that struck you. Let it sink into your heart. What are you feeling about it? What does it mean to you? Write down your thoughts and feelings.

Oratio:	Form your thoughts and feelings into a one-sentence prayer, lifting your thoughts and feelings to the Lord and asking for healing, fullness, or insight.
Contemplatio:	Sit in silence for at least three minutes, opening yourself to the triune Presence. If your mind wanders, bring it back with a word or phrase. Focus on being open and listening.

If you find the Latin of *lectio divina* intimidating, try using the rhythm of the following prayer pattern. This rhythm will allow you to hear God's word for you. Repeat your word or phrase throughout the day to allow yourself to remain in God's presence.

Slow down your reading of your chosen scripture passage.

Listen for the word or phrase that can focus your prayer.

Lift up your word or phrase to God in prayer.

Sink down into the silence of wordless communication with God.

Either *lectio divina* or the prayer pattern above will lead you into scripture and into a deeper way of listening to God. Sometimes the scripture passages you use will raise questions, and you will want to explore the passage further. If you have not done much Bible study, a helpful resource is Rick Warren's *Personal Bible Study Methods*. The book introduces twelve different ways to study scripture and helps identify a good way to explore the biblical texts. One or more of the methods will fit with your way of studying scripture. The discipline of reading and studying the Bible undergirds the other spiritual disciplines and deepens the ability to hear God's leading.

Using *lectio divina* and Bible study as prayer resources can help us become more attentive to the signals God sends to us. We are able to become more aware of our feelings and body reactions which are evoked through the process of opening up to God's Word. That awareness enhances our attentive attitude and openness to God's presence.

———————

The various methods, or disciplines, Christians have developed are available to us as means to enhance our own walk with God and our own journey of faith. The spiritual disciplines provide paths to explore new territory. The disciplines encourage us to enter into conversation with God and to become receptive to God's leading.

CHAPTER 4

Naming and Framing

DECISION MAKING isn't easy. Especially when a decision comes at a crucial point in our lives, we struggle to know how to choose. If we have made poor choices in the past or have come to regret a decision we made, then we may approach important decisions with uncertainty and even fear.

In this chapter we begin to address the ways decisions can be made from a different direction or perspective than you may have used in the past. We begin with a sincere desire to include God in our decision-making efforts, to listen for divine direction, and to find God's longing for us in this particular decision. So, how do we begin this section of the discernment process? What do we do after we have worked through our assumptions and our ongoing relationship with God?

Naming an Issue

We start by naming "the issue" we are facing that calls for a decision. Whether that issue has come up within us or from outside pressures in work or relationships, we face decisions to make and matters to resolve. Perhaps the particular challenge derives from a force over which we have little control, such as an unreasonable boss, a difficult coworker, or even loss of a job. Perhaps the issue involves a difficult relationship with a spouse or child. Or the issue could be a nudging from God about something we need to shift or change in our life. Naming the issue is how we identify it. The activities on pages 53–54 will aid in naming your issue.

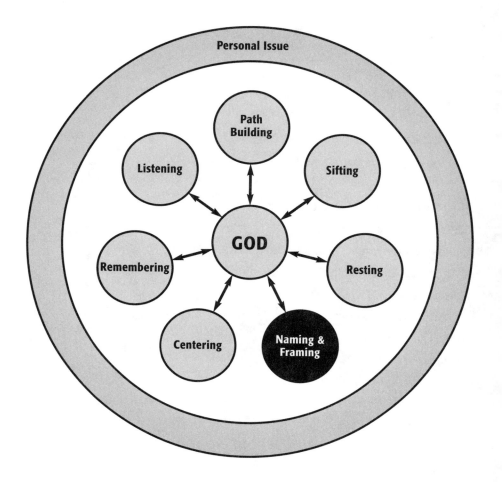

Once you have named the issue you wish to explore in this process, you can begin to refine and focus it. The challenge is to see this particular area of your life from God's perspective. Ask the question: What does God want me to do with _____ (the issue)? The next step is to begin to listen through prayer.

The way of discernment starts with prayer. Because we often have difficulty sorting the voices that come to us from many directions, we ask for God's active presence in the midst of our listening. Spiritual discernment is a gift of God surrounded by grace. When we enter the process without praying for guidance, we are attempting to keep the control ourselves, and perhaps we are even trying to avoid God's leading. The following prayer suggestions direct us toward placing divine guidance in the center of decision making.

Stop and pray. Turn the issue or decision you are facing over to God. Ask for the wisdom of the Holy Spirit to guide you and for the peace of Christ that surpasses all understanding to surround you.

Write your prayer below. Come back to it often as a reminder that you are not alone in this process. The Holy Spirit is your constant companion as you seek to discern God's longing for your life.

If you know someone who has experience in prayer and who keeps prayer requests confidential, ask him or her to pray for you as you walk this journey. This person does not need to know specifics. You may simply say, "I am entering into a time of spiritual discernment and exploration and would deeply appreciate your prayers for guidance, wisdom, courage, and an open mind, heart, eyes, and ears."

As you proceed to clarify the issue or decision you are focusing on, start by describing all the parts within it for which you desire God's guidance. As you begin to identify these different elements, you will also find more clarity about where to focus, where to begin in making your decision.

Naming and Describing the Issue
Ask yourself the following questions:

What is the decision for which I am seeking guidance?

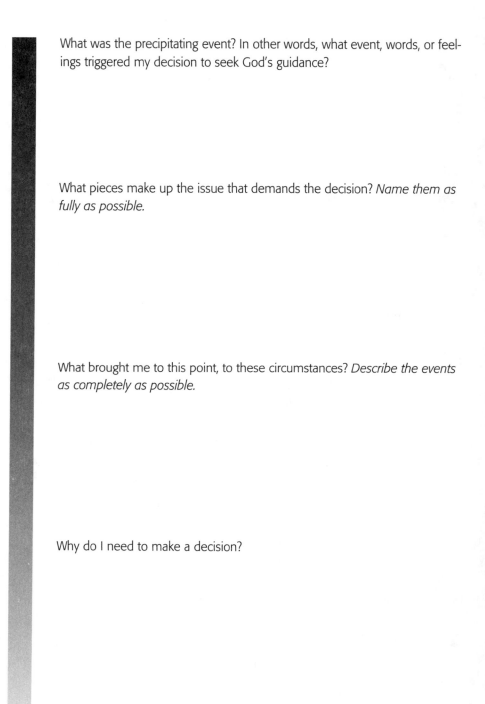

What was the precipitating event? In other words, what event, words, or feelings triggered my decision to seek God's guidance?

What pieces make up the issue that demands the decision? *Name them as fully as possible.*

What brought me to this point, to these circumstances? *Describe the events as completely as possible.*

Why do I need to make a decision?

Framing the Questions

Val is a meditative landscape photographer. She cuts the mats for her work and frames her photographs. Through this process, she has realized that the color and shape of the mat, the process by which she "frames" the picture, either highlights or hides aspects in the picture. Thus, she can evoke different responses from viewers by adjusting how the picture is framed. The same is true for "framing" the questions for discernment. Sometimes we will find that as we change the question, the answers become clearer.

If your issue is *Shall I leave my job or not?* the questions should open up ways to listen to God for leadership in addressing the issue (*How is God yearning for a shift in my work?*). In framing the issue, first we try to identify the broad, overarching questions, such as: *How could I network with people who might shed some light on the dynamics in my job?* Then we can begin to narrow the questions. We will be refining the questions and listening for God's leadership along the way. Perhaps we will ask questions like: *What are the elements in my job that I enjoy? What parts cause me difficulty? How can I begin to shift the emphasis in my work?*

Note that these questions are not yes-or-no questions. God most often has both/and answers to yes-or-no questions. If we leave ourselves open to God's leading, even in the midst of asking the questions, often God sends us into areas we have not considered.

Asking the questions seems like an easy way to begin. And the first questions we ask may be easy. However, as we allow God to reshape the questions, we will respond by changing them to match God's intentions more closely. Unfortunately, we like to think in linear fashion. We try to move clearly from point A to point B—and to finish quickly. However, discernment is not linear, and we may well change the questions and even the focus of the issue as we listen to God's leading.

We live in an instant society, and we often expect quick answers to our questions. Some have said we live in a microwave society. But when we compare the flavor of food heated in a microwave to food prepared in a slow cooker or oven, we notice the richer flavors that develop in the latter. In the same way, the discernment process takes time and is intended to enable us to explore our lives more deeply, to find more complexity and richness inside ourselves, and to be led by God into new discoveries. We cannot expect to receive instant answers to our questions. We need to expect the questions we develop to lead us into complexity.

Name the issue with which you are dealing:

What questions have you discovered pertaining to this issue?

As you work on your questions, continue to refine them again and again, until you feel you have some clarity with your issue. Once you have a good feeling about the questions, live with them for a while. Even if you think you have refined the issue and the questions as much as you possibly can, you may find that they continue to shift a bit as you delve into God's longing.

Here is an example of Val's experience of refining the questions:

When Val attended a denominational meeting, she was intent upon the issue of how best to do the networking possible during such a meeting. The issue was both the number of people to be contacted and the quality of the resulting relationships. She knew she wanted people to learn that Water in the Desert Ministries exists as an organization and what our work entails.

The questions she asked at the beginning were: *God, how am I ever going to know how to network with these people? Who are the most effective contacts to talk to? God, please give me the energy to meet all these people and tell them who we are.* The prospect of networking and finding the appropriate people seemed overwhelming and energy-depleting.

However, as the airplane was landing, the questions suddenly shifted in her mind. All of a sudden, the request became: *God, please place in my path the people you want me to meet and talk to. God, allow me to listen to you so that I am attentive to the people around me during the meeting.* This request allowed her to go with the flow of God's leading and took much less energy than the first set of questions would have done. The focus moved from her initiating the actions to being open to and watching for God's actions.

God indeed put in her path the denominational leaders she needed to tell about our particular ministry. She returned from the meeting energized and focused on the ways to continue networking, rather than returning exhausted from an effort to find people to tell about the organization.

Our questions and requests do shift as we allow God to lead us into the complexities of our issue. The answers to these questions, and the questions themselves, will shed light on God's desire for us. One foundational question undergirds the whole process: God, what are you yearning for me to do with _(the issue)___? All the other questions grow out of this central question.

Mark this section. As you work yourself into the issue and follow the process, you will often find you have asked the wrong questions. Perhaps you need more contemplation and reflection. Thus, you will need to come back to this chapter and re-form the questions once again!

CHAPTER 5

Centering

NOW THAT we have framed our issue by asking questions, we need to become aware of the values and assumptions that affect our process of discernment. This chapter provides guidance for centering ourselves in God's yearning for us and uncovering presuppositions that shape our life.

All of us deal with gravity every day. It is what keeps us solidly on the ground. When our center of gravity is thrown off balance, we fall. When our weight moves too far in one direction or the other without a counterbalance, we run into trouble. Discernment is similar, but instead of gravity keeping us grounded, Christ is our center. When we shift the balance one way or another, based on how we feel or what we value, we move from that center and thus from where the triune God would lead us.

We emphasize again that discernment involves focusing on what God wants. We need to explore new ways to open up our decision-making process. As we observe our process of decision making, we can ask whether or not we are centered in God's guidance or looking elsewhere for guidance—from something or someone other than God.

Core Values

One important aspect of centering ourselves for spiritual discernment involves our core values. They are the values we have developed over the years that serve as pillars of our faith and life. If job security is a core value, then I will say, "Of

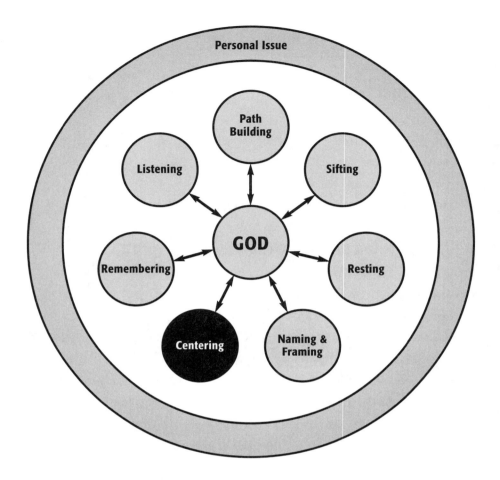

course, I will need to have another job before I can leave this one." Whatever my issue may be, when I say to myself or others, "Of course, I will need to _____," the blank probably is filled with a core value.

Our values are critical to us as we live our lives. As guiding principles, they instruct us on how we live. However, the core values we hold so dearly may not be what God values. We may need to loosen our hold on the bedrock of our values in order to hear God's voice calling us into new arenas. We need to identify the core values that will be significant as we seek answers to the question we have framed.

Richard M. Gula has addressed the ways we have received and become aware of our core values in his book *Moral Discernment*. He explains that we receive the values we use in moral decision making from three contexts: social, situational, and personal. "We cannot be completely autonomous in making a moral choice because the social realities that surround us strongly influence our sense of value and virtue."[1] As we become aware of how we have been influenced in the religious arena—by the Bible, Jesus, and the church—and in the social arena—by communities, role models, and expert authorities, we begin to see where we received the values we have internalized.

The formative dimensions that have gone into the development of our decision-making abilities shape the conscience we rely on. The convictions of conscience and the moral obligations we live by have been learned within the communities that have influenced us. Our sources of moral wisdom include family, friends, colleagues, and experts as well as the broader communities of Christian sources, such as the Bible, theologians, teachers, and any pastoral mentoring we have experienced. As we work with our core values, we need to identify as many sources as we can. With that knowledge we can put into perspective the elements that have shaped our conscience and convictions.

Jesus says, "Not my will but yours be done."
—Luke 22:42

Not all these sources will have been positive influences in our lives. If we have experienced abuse of trust from influential people, lack of mature moral decisions, or interpretations of the Bible that lead to a narrow moral stance, we may have formed a value system in response to these negative events. In order to explore this portion of our faith journey, we need to name those influences and experiences and identify their impact on us.

Now that we have looked at the sources of our core values, it is time to begin naming them. Here are some examples of categories in which we form core values.

- Biblical and theological foundations—how we approach the Bible and apply it in life
- Integrity—how we define living and working above reproach
- Family—how we spend time and energy on nurture and development of our family
- Money—how the way we make and spend money reflects our priorities
- Contribution to society—the ways we give time to issues in the larger community

Within any category, each of us develops our core values from our own background. The values are evident in the choices we make in our lives. Use this list to begin naming your core values. As you work through the process of discernment you probably will add to them.

What core values are important to me as I follow this path of spiritual discernment?

Which core value seems to rise to the surface as the most important one to use as a guiding principle in my discernment process?

We need to emphasize once again that clarifying and sorting our core values is difficult. When we come to realize that a cherished value is *mine* but not God's, it may be easier for us to let it go if God calls us to do that. As we begin to live a life of discernment, we may find our priorities are changing; our core values are shifting in intensity and moving closer to God's values. Changes do happen, and we are called to reflect upon where we need to let go of once-cherished values and beliefs.

One of Judith's core values is maintaining a neat, clean house. She reflects:

> As I have explored this value, I have come to realize I incorporated the value into my life from my grandparents and parents, and from my Midwestern middle-class upbringing. As I work with Habitat for Humanity, I realize that other values are more important to people who have grown up in different places with different parental influences and social locations. Although we both own houses and value the role of homeowner, others may not "keep"

the house in a way that matches my core value. If I judge the other person on how neat his or her house is, I hold my set of values around neatness to be more important than the personhood of the other.

Once I have figured out that another's values may differ from mine, I still can hold the value for myself. But I hold it lightly, knowing that it is mine and not God's. In my study of the Bible I have come to understand that God considers relationships with people more important than the neatness of my house. Perhaps in my journey I may even learn to listen to another's values in a way that shifts my own and refocuses my discernment issue.

Perhaps the examination of my core value allows me to move into an understanding of the biblical challenge for stewardship. I may well grow to understand that I hold the property as God's gift and therefore am steward for the long-term value and livability of the house. This attitude changes my priorities and shifts my understanding from being "owner" to being "steward." Thus, as I enter into a discernment question regarding whether or not I leave this house, I can be open to move away from it because the house I am leaving is not mine but God's. And as I look at new houses I can see them as ones of which I could be a steward rather than an owner. This shift in values may open up new possibilities that lie before me.

We name our core values so that they can be instructive to us and available to God for change. Unless we participate in naming and in opening ourselves to the possibility of change, it will be hard to remain centered in God. Our values speak so loudly that we will have trouble hearing God's longing for our lives. In order to see and shift long-held values, we must give the whole discernment process to God and say, like Jesus, "yet not my will but yours be done" (Luke 22:42).

Holy Indifference

The principle of holy indifference was named in the sixteenth century by Ignatius of Loyola in his classic text *Spiritual Exercises. Holy indifference* is a positive stance in the process of centering. Ignatian indifference can be described as a state of inner freedom, openness, and balance. It does not incline us more toward one option than another. Instead, this indifference "is a poised freedom that preserves our ability to go one way or another depending on God's lead. By calling for indifference, Ignatius is calling for a willingness right from the start to be influenced in the process by God's guidance."[2]

This way of being can also be called *shedding*, which is defined as "naming and laying aside anything that will deter the person or group from focusing on God's will as the ultimate value."[3] Shedding involves letting go of our agendas and becoming indifferent to any choice *except* what God wants. It sounds easy, but it's not!

Usually we are taught not to be indifferent to actions going on around us but to be actively involved in managing and controlling the decisions in our life. So when we hear we must become indifferent to the outcome, especially when it involves a personal issue, we resist. Our initial reaction may be to raise questions: *What do you mean I shouldn't care about the outcome of the decision concerning my issue? I am involved, and I do care about the outcome. How can I be indifferent?*

Holy indifference means not caring about the outcome *except* as God wants the outcome. The point is not to direct the results *except* as God directs. We are to become indifferent to any outcome *except* God's longing for us. The focus shifts, and the way of discernment becomes centered on God.

Holy indifference continues to be demanding throughout the discernment journey because we bump up against presuppositions we may have held for a long time. We need to notice what is difficult to let go of in order to follow God's yearning for our life. The places where we say "yes, but" indicate we've come up against a presupposed belief. The content of the "but" shows us where our fears and insecurities lie and where we need to begin working. Developing holy indifference requires us to assume anything other than God's yearning is not where we want to go with our issue.

If we write down the "yes, but" places, they can become part of the exploration process. For example, if I am looking around for another job, then perhaps I will say something like: "God, I will move anywhere you want, except Denver, Colorado." Or, "I will take any job you open up for me, except being a school principal." Whatever is the content of the phrase beginning with "except" will help us see the points where we hesitate to follow God's leading. Why not move anywhere God wants? Why not take any job God wants me to take? We will probably find a whole list of good reasons not to do what we are afraid God wants us to do.

Holy indifference challenges us to let go of each of those exceptions, one by one, until we are ready to understand deeply that no matter where God calls us, God has considered all our objections. No matter what our fears or objections are, if God calls us into that situation, God has good and sufficient reasons for the call; and we will be given strength for the journey.

God calls us to let go of our objections, to let go of our fears, to trust so deeply that God's yearning and Christ's call to us will be enough. We will be surrounded and supported by the Holy Spirit in ways that empower us to move through our fears to our trust in God's sufficiency. We are called upon to face our fears and to examine what holds us back from walking with boldness into God's future. We are called upon to trust at a level that is new territory for many of us. We are encouraged to enter into a more profound relationship with God than we may have thought possible. All these struggles come running to surround us as soon as we begin to allow God to have a major voice in our decision making.

As you work through centering your issue and questions in God's yearning for you, note your places of resistance.

What am I having a hard time letting go of?
Write down all the "exceptions" that prevent you from reaching holy indifference in the context of your named issue.

Write a prayer asking for God's help and grace in reaching a place of holy indifference to any outcome except God's longing for you. You probably will need to repeat this prayer on a regular basis.

CHAPTER 6

Remembering

STORYTELLING has been an influential part of human history. Stories are passed down from generation to generation by grandparents, parents, and storytellers in communities. Storytelling reminds us who we are; and for the community of faith, stories remind us to whom we belong. Stories are used as a means to pass history on to each successive generation, for teaching purposes, and, of course, for entertainment. The act of telling becomes a way to "re-member" the event, to put all the pieces back together so that we bring a past event into our present.

Remembering helps us know where we've been and who we were. Val remembers: When I was growing up, "history lessons" were always a part of family dinners, especially if we had company. My father was always teaching us through family stories. We heard tales of ancestors whom we had never met. We learned about the early days of our grandparents, aunts, and uncles; and these people came alive to us. More significantly, we learned where our family had come from and what it meant to be a member of this particular family. The stories were entertaining, but they also allowed us to bring to life (re-member) those events that had shaped our history.

You may be asking, *What does this have to do with discernment?* As the old saying goes, "We can't know where we are going if we don't know where we have been." Looking at the path we have trod in order to arrive at this place, remembering when we have called on God, when we have felt God's presence acting in our lives, and when we have felt God's absence are important steps in

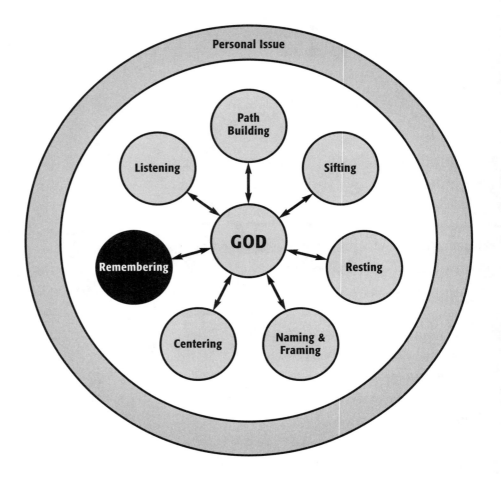

knowing where God is leading us. Thus, remembering our stories helps us place the focus of our questions in the context of our lives and the life of the community of faith around us.

Maureen Conroy reminds us that "God's touch, though taking place in a moment of time, lives on within us forever."[1] When we remember the times we have experienced God, we reenact those events in our heart and mind. They remind us of God's grace and love and the fact that we are not alone. The remembering brings to a conscious level that which has touched our lives in the past. We are reminded that we are children of God and that we are beloved (see chapter 2). God has touched us and led us in the past, and God will be faithful to do so in the present and future.

Whatever our experiences with the presence or absence of God, they need to be heard in context of the community of faith. Hearing stories of how God has acted in the lives of others affirms, challenges, and elicits our own stories.

Biblical Call to Remember

We encounter the call to remember God's mighty acts throughout the Bible. That theme permeates the book of Deuteronomy, especially in chapters 8 and 9 when Moses called the Israelites to recall all that God had done for them. As they anticipated settling into the land, they were challenged not to forget who had acted in their lives to bring them out of slavery in Egypt and into the Promised Land.

Often the distractions of our personal lives cause us to forget to whom we belong and who has acted mightily in our lives. Exodus and Joshua give instructions to remember and to retell the story of God's actions. Exodus 12 describes Passover as an act of remembrance, and verse 26 specifically instructs people to tell the story of God's faithfulness when children ask about the meaning of the observance.

In Joshua 4 the people are told to take twelve stones from the Jordan River and place them as a memorial. When the children ask what the stones are for, the people tell the story of how God cut off the waters of the Jordan River to let the people pass through on dry land (Josh. 4:4-7).

The Psalms are also full of remembrance and the charge not to forget. Many psalms recall God's faithfulness to the community of faith or the individual. Some call on God not to forget the relationship with God's people. Other psalms retell the community's history emphasizing the theme of remembrance. The Psalms were intended to be repeated over and over to remind us of God's leading in the past, of God's faithfulness, and of God's love and grace. In the Psalms we are reminded that we are not alone and that God will act in our future as we discern God's longing for us.

Christians partake in similar acts of remembrance during the year as we celebrate the major events in our shared history: Christmas, Easter, and Pentecost. With each of these religious holidays we retell the story of God's interaction with us. We also participate in a dynamic remembering each time we come to

I will call to mind the deeds of the LORD; I will remember your wonders of old, I will meditate on all your work, and muse on your mighty deeds. Your way, O God, is holy.

—Psalm 77:11-13

the Lord's Table to celebrate Communion. In Luke 22:19 Jesus says, "This is my body, which is given for you. Do this in remembrance of me." Therefore, every time we come together around the communion table, we "re-member" that night when Jesus had supper with the community of men and women around him. We tell the story and remember all the meaning wrapped up in that simple, yet complex, event.

Personal Stories

The following exercises offer a way to start putting your own story into words in the context of God's faithfulness.

Use the next several minutes to stop and think about your life and then answer the following questions.

- What were the major turning points in my life?

- How did I feel God's presence in my life at these times?

- When else in my life have I felt God's faithfulness or presence?

- When have I sought God's guidance in the past? What did I do and how did God answer?

- When have I felt God's absence? What did I do then, and how did God's silence feel?

Remember and write your story as it leads to the issue you have lifted up for discernment:

Through this exercise, we have responded to the biblical call to remember what God has done in our life. We have also listened to our own personal story as it relates God's interaction in our life. Now it is time to move into a broader community to hear the stories that are part of its history. This broader community involves stories from the Bible and from ancestors in our faith, such as Ignatius, Teresa of Ávila, John Calvin, John Wesley, Mother Teresa, and the people around us, especially in our churches.

The Community of Faith

Our stories need to be placed in the context of the community of faith. We need to tell our stories, and we need to hear other people's stories. The dynamic of these two storytelling streams—hearing the stories of others and telling our own stories—leads toward the possible paths ahead of us. We can be challenged to think outside the box or to let go of old notions. The voices of others can also elucidate our foundational understandings. Allowing our lives to intersect with these stories can also bring to mind events of God's faithfulness in our lives that we have forgotten.

The Bible is a source and place to begin when listening and remembering the stories of the community of faith. It testifies to God's faithfulness, to our actions as human beings, and to our interactions with the triune God. It is alive, and we can find ourselves in the text. The Bible is full of what we call *paradigm stories*. These are the ones in which we see the issues of our ancestors repeated in the issues of our lives today. Hearing the paradigm stories recorded in the Bible, of those humans who have gone before us, sheds light on the issue at hand.

Often people say to us, "But I don't know any biblical stories that apply to my own story." Here are ways you can find those stories:

- *Read the Bible on a regular basis.* You will become more familiar with the stories, and they will begin to inform your journey. A lectionary is a wonderful tool to help focus your Bible reading.
- *Use* lectio divina *(chapter 3) to bring the stories alive.*
- *Ask your pastor or spiritual director for help* in identifying stories that speak to your situation in life.

The stories of ancestors in our faith, such as the desert fathers and mothers or the mystics, may also open up new avenues of exploration. Many of these stories can be found on the Internet if you do not have access to a theological library. Or read about individuals who shaped your own denomination. Many people find it fruitful to recall the stories of people whom they have met in their church or over the course of their lives. Listening to their stories and journeys of faith becomes yet another way to listen to God's longing for your future.

You are not being asked to mimic these stories or take the paths others have taken. You are invited to let their stories of faithfulness fan the spark of God's presence in your life as you are inspired and encouraged by others.

What biblical story or stories come to mind at this stage in my journey of spiritual discernment? How do they relate to my situation?

How does the biblical text bring new insights to my journey of faith?

What other stories within the broader community of faith speak to me?

How do the stories call up forgotten times of God's faithfulness in my life?

How do these stories challenge my thinking?

How do the stories shed light on the issue I'm facing or the question I've framed for spiritual discernment?

Journaling

Throughout this chapter we have discussed remembering and telling stories about the ways God has acted in our lives. Now is an appropriate time to talk about journaling. If you already journal, this section may not offer new insights, but if journaling has not been a part of your faith journey, take time to read this section.

Keeping a journal can prepare the way for spiritual discernment. A personal journal is a place and an opportunity to record thoughts, questions, joys, concerns, struggles, and prayers, as well as reflections upon God's actions. Once these reflections are written down, it is easy to review them later with a fresh perspective. When we review entries after a lapse of time, we often recognize interactions with God. In retrospect we can see God's faithfulness in our life and identify how God was leading us. Journaling also brings clarity to our focus and questions as we work through feelings and facts on paper.

You may be asking, *What do I write in a journal and how do I begin?* There is no right or wrong way to journal. The process that works for you is the "right" process. You may find that the ways you journal change over time. Give yourself grace. Don't force what doesn't work. As with other parts of your life, invite God into your journaling.

Since you are working on spiritual discernment, start by recording your answers to the questions in this workbook. As you become comfortable writing down your feelings in the discernment process, you will begin to journal about other areas of your life. Include the questions you have for God or about God. Record your struggles and how you worked through them or how you still struggle. Write down joys, blessings, and thanksgivings. Take the time to write down how you see God acting in your life or the lives of others. If you sense God is absent, write about the experience. If a biblical passage speaks to you, put it in your journal and write your thoughts concerning the passage. As you can see, what you put in the journal depends on you.

Remember, this is not school! You don't have to turn in the journal to anyone to read or grade. What you write remains private and doesn't have to be shared with anyone unless you wish. That is your choice.

Journaling takes many forms. Some people are committed to pen and paper, while others couldn't journal without a computer. Journals may include drawings or doodling, since both often reflect feelings. Writing poetry is another way to express your feelings and God's activities. There are no rules about time frame or frequency of journaling. Some people feel something is missing if they don't write every day. Others turn to journaling when they are especially happy or troubled.

Let the process begin with a prayer. Write with grace and review the journal to remember where God has been faithful.

CHAPTER 7

Listening

NOW THE TIME has come to focus attention on a more formalized process of listening. We will gather data and opinions that have an impact upon our decision making. We have been listening to a variety of voices before reaching this circle. Here we will pull together both factual information and feelings. Our listening will move to a deeper level.

"Let anyone with ears to hear listen!" Jesus says in Mark 4:9. Many people heard Jesus' words, but only those who were willing to let those words soak into their very being were able to listen to his message. In this circle we are asked to open our ears and allow the many voices around us to surface and speak to us. This kind of listening may seem confusing, because the voices we hear will have different opinions about our issue and decisions. Fears do arise at this point as we open ourselves to others' opinions and our own internal voices. We need the centering provided by our walk through previous circles. It is appropriate to stop and pray a prayer like the following:

> Loving God, full of compassion and grace, walk beside me as I begin to listen to all the voices and to collect information I will use in discerning your longing for me. I am afraid that I will listen to the wrong voices or that I won't hear the voices I need to hear. Open my ears to hear. Assuage my fears and help me resist blocking the voices I don't want to hear. May the Holy Spirit grant me wisdom. In the name of the One who challenged me to hear, Jesus Christ my Savior, Amen.

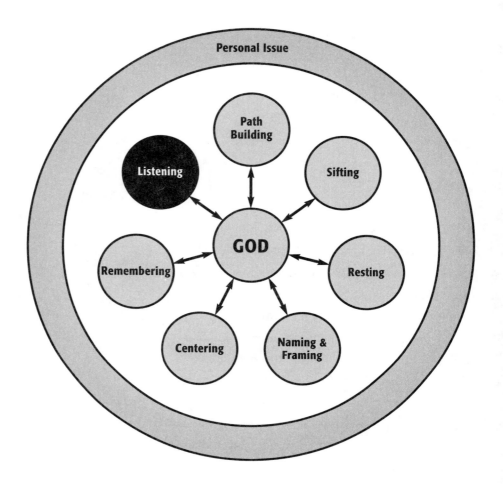

Data Gathering

Begin to gather the information from various places and organize it in the chart on page 80. The chart helps you sort out the voices: voices with facts and data, voices of other people, interior voices and feelings, and voices from other sources. Continue to categorize information you discover about the subject of your discernment. Add the voices to the chart by listing the facts as you know them, talking to other people, listening to interior thoughts and feelings, and paying attention to the other "voices," such as music, art, and the written word.

You will not make your final decision based solely on the chart. The chart just facilitates recording and laying out in visual form what you are hearing. You will use this information in the next chapter as you begin to build the possible paths.

In the process of recording the voices, it is important to separate "you" messages from "I" messages. The "you" messages come when others tell you what you should or ought to do or be. The "I" messages come from what you have integrated for yourself. "You should . . ." is quite a different message than "I want. . . ." When you record what other people are saying, listen carefully both to what they say and to how they word their message to you. As you try to separate out your own knowledge and understanding, make sure to include the pronoun "I" to remind yourself that these insights come from your knowledge and feelings, not necessarily what another knows and feels.

Instructions for Using the Chart

Now that you have a method for recording your data, it is time to begin to record what you have gathered. Add facts, voices, and feelings as they come to bear upon your questions. The chart will grow and expand as you fill out each of the boxes. You will want to make copies of the chart so that you can add to it, revise, or start fresh as you go along.

QUESTION

Write out the question or questions as you have framed it/them regarding the issue or decision you are facing.

VOICES COLUMN

Listening to God in the discernment process is not easy. You will hear many other voices as you seek advice and counsel from people. Some voices are from God, and some are not. Notice the voices that echo your own desires and longings. Notice the voices that echo your own fears or the fears of those around you. Identifying the voices that reflect your desires and also the places where you are afraid becomes essential to the process of sorting out and weighing the information you are gathering.

You will take all these voices into consideration when listening for God's direction. Pay attention to the voices and then begin to pray about them to determine what is and is not from God.

WRITE THE QUESTION YOU HAVE FRAMED	
Voices	**Feelings**
The facts as I know them:	I am feeling the following about this issue:
Other people are saying:	I experience these feelings after listening to the people around me:
My interior voices are saying:	I experience these feelings about my interior voices:
Other voices I am hearing through music, art, the Bible and other written words:	I experience these feelings about the other voices I am hearing:

From *Living into the Answers* © 2008 by Valerie K. Isenhower and Judith A. Todd, published by Upper Room Books.
May be reproduced for personal use only.

FEELINGS COLUMN

You have feelings about each of the voices that you identify. Identifying and naming your feelings is also part of the process of listening. This exercise combines head and heart in a way that facilitates the sorting process.

THE FACTS AS I KNOW THEM

What are the facts concerning the focus question of your discernment? When you start filling out the listening process chart, you will already know some facts. But you may need to do a bit of research. Some "facts" are feeling-based and intuitive; you may need to look more carefully at them. You may find something you thought was a fact is not. Just because you've "always been told that" doesn't ensure reliability. Keep track of what you are learning on your chart.

For example, let's say you're asking, *God, what are you yearning for me to do with my job?* You might list facts such as the following:

- I need to change jobs.
- My boss hates me.
- I am better at doing X than I am doing my current job.

Separate the facts from your feelings.

> I need to change jobs—
> *factual reasons*: financial, location, family pressures, layoffs
> *feelings*: dissatisfaction, fear, feeling incapable, longing for more
> or greater fulfillment

You may move between the facts and how you feel about the facts. Let the two columns in each row inform your exploration. Remember this is a time for identifying as much data as possible. The sorting and prioritizing process comes later. Continue to return to these boxes as other pieces of information present themselves during your exploration.

OTHER PEOPLE ARE SAYING

What are the people around you saying as it relates to your situation? Write down their responses to your questions in the chart. Continue to identify people you could talk to. The following questions can point you toward individuals who may offer valuable insights on the issue:

- Who is directly involved in your situation, such as family members or close friends?

- Who are the advisers you trust?

- Who do you consider to be a wise person or one with good insights?

- Who will hold your process in confidence, especially if you are dealing with an issue from work, school, or church?

- Who holds some information you need to take into consideration?

- Who does God want you to talk to? Ask the Holy Spirit to bring these people across your path, and watch for people who come to you in unexpected ways during this process.

The list will change as you proceed. If you choose to broadcast your question for discernment to your entire community of friends, relatives, and colleagues, listening to everyone probably will cloud the issue. You may have too many voices and too many opinions to lend clarity. If you talk with everyone, try to sort the voices into groups with similar responses. In this way, you may be able to make the range of responses more manageable.

You do need to find supportive people with whom to share the journey of discernment and discovery. Retaining your balance while listening to other voices can be a tricky enterprise. The voices will pull first one way, then another way, and the result may well become quite confusing. But you will find a rhythm to gathering the voices and then moving apart from the voices in order to sort them out. Don't forget to record how you are feeling about the voices as you listen.

While the listening process continues, remember you are not asking these people to live your life but to assist you in reflecting upon your issue. The final decision is between you and God. Turn to God as your center when the voices upset your balance and cause confusion.

My Interior Voices Are Saying

What are the voices inside you saying about the issue? These interior voices are the tapes you have internalized, such as

- I should . . .
- I shouldn't . . .

- My family always . . .
- Men don't . . . OR Men do . . .
- Women don't . . . OR Women do . . .
- Christians don't . . . OR Christians do . . .

As you listen to and explore these voices, you will hear bits and pieces of your own story. The encounters with your life experiences will lead you into remembering times of joy and release. You may also recall traumatic events and struggles from your past. Long-held fears, feelings of guilt and anger, or frustration over lost opportunities may open up. Return to God as your center when those feelings from the past resurface.

LISTENING TO THE PEOPLE AROUND ME

Begin now to listen to a variety of voices around you. God's word comes to us in many forms—voices of people, music, art, and written words. Notice the voices you perceive as authoritative. Realize that God may be using new ways to speak to you at this time. God may very well use a person you don't normally listen to or someone you don't even know to bring you a message. Sometimes a voice may be subtle. God does get our attention, although not always by means of a burning bush (see Exod. 3). God often chooses to use the still small voice (1 Kings 19).

Ask yourself the following questions to become more aware of what influences you.

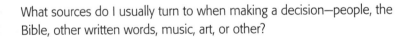

What sources do I usually turn to when making a decision—people, the Bible, other written words, music, art, or other?

How do these ways of listening influence me?

How do I gain guidance from them?

On which modes of communication do I place most importance?

FEARS THAT ARISE

What are you afraid of as you listen to the voices? Again, it's important to address your fears. Fears get in the way of uncovering God's yearning for your life.

The fears pop up when we hear a voice and our reaction is "yes, but"; "I couldn't do that, because . . ."; or "but, what if. . . ." The fears arise from our experiences and limit the ways we are able to address our issue. Our fears bind us with their aim to keep us safe from dangerous territory.

God's yearning often calls upon us to set aside our fears and to trust in God alone. Remember when the angels appear and say, "Do not be afraid" (Matt. 1:20; 28:5 and Luke 1:13, 30). In the biblical stories, as well as in our own, God's voice calls us to live on the other side of our fears, to live into God's vision for the future.

Listen to the angels say, "Do not be afraid!"

Say to yourself:
God is with me and will walk with me through the process and will not leave me when the decision is made and I begin to live into God's yearning.

Ask Jesus to walk with you through your fears. Ask God to give you courage and strength to face them, for in so doing you can live into the fullness and abundance God wants for you.

If you are addressing your fears, but they continue to be stumbling blocks, try these strategies:

Review the section on exploring the inward life in chapter 2.

Return to chapter 4 and look again at the issues and questions you have formed. You may need to visit the issue again, addressing your fears as part of that process. Then recast the questions.

Finally, reread the section on holy indifference (chapter 5) and lift your fears up to God. You may need to stop the process here while you and God work on your fears so they will not stand in the way of listening to God.

When our fears are addressed we will have progressed deeper into the process of discerning God's yearning for us. Once again, "addressing our fears" is much easier to talk about than to do. Perhaps the next exercise will help you identify your fears. Once you have pushed underneath the surface and caught a glimpse of your fears, they can be named. It's only after you see and identify them that you can decide what to do with them.

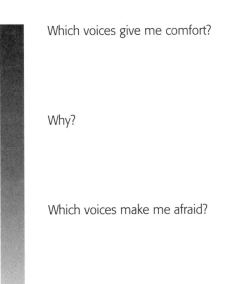

Which voices give me comfort?

Why?

Which voices make me afraid?

Why?

When I think of God's yearning for me, do I ever say, "but what if . . ."? What stirs up that response?

Ask one of your most trusted confidants to pray for guidance and insight as you discover your fears.

The Holy Spirit

As we have seen earlier, direction for God's yearning for our lives comes to us in many forms. The Holy Spirit is active in our process, so be prepared to listen to words from unexpected places and unexpected people. The following story involves Val's response to the prompting of the Holy Spirit:

> I was in a process of discerning my call into ministry. The pastor of the church I was attending asked me to be one of the participants in the Easter sunrise service. I agreed, and although I was comfortable in front of groups, I was a bit nervous about leading in worship. I read my assigned parts during worship and was relieved when my part was completed so I could stop worrying. I hadn't wanted to make a mistake, so I had practiced, practiced, practiced. And now, it was done.

> After the service, when we all headed to the fellowship hall for the traditional Easter breakfast, the person behind me in line began talking to me. He was a new member of the church, and we hadn't had a chance to get acquainted. I was interested in getting to know him, when suddenly he said to me, "You should think about attending seminary and becoming a pastor." I was totally surprised. Since the pastor was the only one who knew where I was in my discernment process, I accused him of prompting this man to encourage my choice for seminary. However, the truth was that this individual felt a prompting from the Holy Spirit to say those words to me.

The Holy Spirit also uses other ways to give us guidance in the process. Often those in discernment say they are caught off guard by the words of a song or portions of a worship service that seem to be speaking directly to them. Ellen Morseth, in her book *Ritual and the Arts in Spiritual Discernment,* talks about using art to assist in the discernment process. She suggests that you find a picture of a path, road, gate, or other meditative image. For example, use the cover image on this workbook for meditation. The picture of the gate, taken by Val, invites you to ask, *Which side of the gate am I on? What is on the other side of the gate? Where is God calling me to be?*

Meditate on the picture. Where do you find yourself in it? Often, your honest response to a piece of art such as this one clarifies the way you are feeling about your issue.

Notice the ways the Holy Spirit prompts interior feelings. Paying attention to how you feel is an important part of discernment. The Holy Spirit will often give you a sense of ease or dis-ease about a decision, so listening to your feelings becomes important. Val describes her experience of an interior prompting from the Holy Spirit:

> I was in the process of deciding whether or not to apply for a job. I had made the initial phone call for data gathering, but my reaction after talking to the person in charge was to forget about the job. The job description wasn't what I really wanted, and the salary was less than I had hoped for. However, as the next several days went by, I realized I couldn't "let go" of it. My thoughts kept returning to the job. It was clear that the Holy Spirit kept prompting me to follow through on the application process. So I continued to listen. I submitted my application and waited for the next step of data gathering—the interview. When the process was completed, I was offered the job, and I accepted the offer. After being on the job for a while, it became clear that indeed God's yearning had been for me to fill that position. I would have missed an opportunity for growth and networking and learning important skills if I hadn't paid attention to the internal feelings from the Holy Spirit. If I hadn't listened, I would have missed the ways that the

THERE ARE a couple of places where you can find artwork for your discernment process. Water in the Desert Ministries and V. Isenhower Photography offer "Focus on Discernment" kits. Each kit includes seven 8½ x 11 inch photographs for discernment, a tabletop easel, a candleholder, questions, and scriptural texts to reflect on while you mediate on the pictures. The kits can be purchased at www.visenhowerphotography.com or www.waterinthedesert.org.

Icons are another source of art that can be helpful. Search the Web for stores that sell icons online or visit a Catholic or Eastern Orthodox bookstore in your area.

experience in the organization and the relationships I developed there prepared me for my current ministry with Water in the Desert Ministries.

Continuing to read biblical stories provides another avenue where the Holy Spirit can prompt us. The spiritual practice of *lectio divina* encourages us to slow down and ponder the words in a passage. The word or words we hear echoing in our lives from the biblical stories we read become a part of the listening process. The Holy Spirit will emphasize words for us as we have the ears and patience to hear.

In chapters 1 and 6 we took note of several biblical stories that speak to our question for discernment. Taking another look at those stories, the Psalms, or other biblical passages allows God's voice to be heard. Use the questions on pages 73–74 to revisit biblical stories and heighten your awareness to the Holy Spirit's promptings.

After listening to the many voices around and within myself, does any biblical story come to mind?

If so, locate the passage and take time to meditate on it (see description of lectio divina *in chapter 3). If no story comes to mind, choose one of the stories explored in chapter 1 or 6 and meditate on it using* lectio divina*. Write your thoughts below:*

The Holy Spirit speaks to us in many ways. Take note of ways the Holy Spirit is speaking to you in addition to what is mentioned in this chapter. Ask yourself, What words are coming to me from unexpected sources like strangers, music, worship, and art?

Are there any feelings I can't let go of at this stage?

Consolidating

By this time your ears are probably tired and you may be on information over-load, especially if you are an introvert. The data gathering and listening circle of the process is challenging and takes time. Trust in God and a spirit of openness. Now, after gathering this data and listening to the voices, it is time to begin consolidating those voices.

Continue to pay attention to the many voices that speak to you about your issue and decision making. The next two chapters focus on *path building* and *sifting*, so the voices will become clearer. At this point, simply look back over your experience in data gathering and notice the major trends or pieces of information that rise to your attention. You'll pay more attention to them as you work through the next circles. You are not weighing the questions/data/answers at this point. The following exercise represents a first round of sorting.

Go back to the chart of "voices" and your notes on the last section, review them, and ask yourself the following questions:

What voices are similar or along the same track?

What voices differ from each other?

Pondering

Before moving on to the next circle in the discernment process, you will ponder the data gathered through listening. Don't rush through this section, because it can hold significant insights and helpful information.

Remember the words in Luke 2:19, "But Mary treasured all these words and pondered them in her heart." The process of pondering the words in your heart gives time and space for new revelations. As you write what the voices say, you begin to experience feelings about them. As you write and ponder, lift the voices up to God along with the entire discernment process.

You have begun to pay attention to your initial reaction to the voices you have heard. Sometimes this "gut reaction" or intuition is accurate and helpful to listen to because it is the Holy Spirit speaking from within you. Yet at other times, these initial reactions block the discernment process because the reaction points you toward your fears.

Each of us has "cover stories" from which we live our lives. These are the surface-level stories we tell others and ourselves. These cover stories allow us to live in self-deception, and they block us from living into wholeness. For example, you tell your children you can't go to Disneyland because it is too expensive, when in reality you don't want to go because you know you will have to get on the rides, and you are deathly afraid of the rides. Your cover story is the expense of the trip, but your real story is your fear of the rides.

If we will acknowledge our own "real story" and allow God into the midst of it, transformation can happen. In the case above, if we can be honest with our children, they may well suggest a creative solution that would allow the trip to happen and in so doing provide a priceless family experience. (For more information on cover stories and self-deception, see Dan Via's book *Self-Deception and Wholeness in Paul and Matthew*.)

The same principle holds true in the discernment process. Often we will only listen to the voices that allow us to stay within the boundaries of our cover story. We don't want to take a new job because we are fearful that we might fail, so we listen only to the voices telling us not to take the job. We often have difficulty identifying our cover story because we are invested in it and believe it to be the real story. We do not identify our fears but keep them hidden for as long as possible. Our fears are based in our own early experiences, observation of others' disasters, or what we've been taught. Our cover story helps us cope with life and is deeply embedded in our understanding of who we are. Ask yourself some questions that enable you to identify your cover story; also ask yourself about places where the voices encourage you to stay within that story.

Defining areas of self-deception and our cover stories means facing our fears again.

In the context of your issue—
Remember one or two early life experiences that made you afraid.
I'm afraid because . . .

Name another person's experience you have observed that affects how you handle your own issue in a negative way.
[For example: "I know someone who moved away from family to take a new job. The person got homesick, quit the job, moved home, and took a job for less pay. I'm afraid the same thing will happen to me. Therefore, I'll never take a job in another state."]

I'll never do (*action*) regarding (*my issue*) because I am afraid (*describe your fear[s]*).

Explore an area related to your issue where you were taught to avoid an action. [For example: "I've heard you should never drop out of college before completing your degree because you'll never go back to school."]

I'll never _(action)_ because disaster is bound to follow.

Review your answers and ponder this question:
Where am I living in self-deception and allowing my fears to prevent hearing God's yearning?

What practices, such as prayer, scripture reading, or meditation, might allow God's healing or direction to penetrate my cover story?

CHAPTER 8

Path Building

YOU HAVE SPENT a lot of time naming issues, framing and perhaps reframing the questions, remembering, and listening. Now you are ready to begin pulling everything together. At this stage in your journey, you need to look at the possible paths available based on all the information you have gathered to date. It is time to let your imagination loose, to be creative and not limit God's possibilities. Don't discount anything. Let your dreams range as widely as possible.

The information you have gathered probably sorts itself into several major categories we can call "paths." Each path represents a different direction you could take to resolve your issue or to make your decision. Each path has advantages and disadvantages, strengths and weaknesses, good outcomes and challenges. Before you choose among the options—or paths—consider each one in turn. In the process of following a path or option to the point where it resolves your issue, you may find one or more ways that open up with exciting possibilities. Let your imaginative abilities play with the alternatives before you close off the options.

Before proceeding further, though, we need to absorb what it means "to let your *imagination* loose." We are talking about the God-given creative spirit that receives guidance from the Holy Spirit. God's vision and creative powers are so awesome and so big that unless we tap into the creative place inside us led by the Holy Spirit, we will limit our view of the possibilities God sets before us. Thus, when we talk about letting your imagination loose, we mean to open

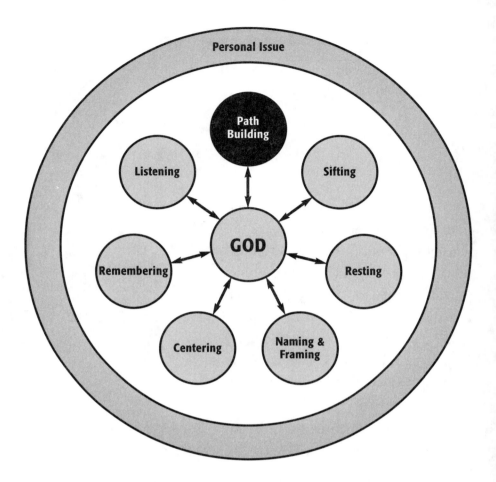

yourself up to the Holy Spirit, to allow the creative powers of the Spirit to guide you in thinking of paths you could never dream about otherwise.

Which Paths Are Possible?

We continue to identify and refine what we know and what we can dream. We have gathered lots of information, listened to many voices and thought many thoughts. Now we need to put the thoughts and voices into some kind of order. We don't need to weed out ideas yet. We do need to study what we know already, and to begin to pull some of the pieces together.

Make several copies of the template on page 95. Write one option at the top of the template, then describe the steps needed to build the path to achieve

Option # ___

Briefly describe this option.

Build on the option. Describe the path ahead of you by listing each of the steps needed to achieve the option.

Where does this path lead?

Where does this path begin to come to an end, and what is the conclusion?

Is this path similar to any of the other paths? How?

Where does it differ from other paths?

How do you feel about this option? List your fears, joys, and concerns:

the option. Do this in a manner that seems easiest: write a story, draw a diagram, or simply list each step of the path. Be sure to include important information and any stops along the way.

The point is to name the options, to see where each path is leading, and then to see how this life direction will affect the issue you have identified for exploration. You will begin to see the possibilities open up or close down before you. After you have completed this exercise for one path, repeat it for all the other possible options and paths.

For example, if your issue centers around your job and whether you are going to leave the position you have now, possible options may be

- to look for another job in the same field;
- to look for more training;
- to look for a job in a related field;
- to apprentice with a master;
- to switch fields entirely;
- to go to school.

The more options you open up and consider, the better for discernment. Next, begin to define the steps that lead toward the various options. This is path building. Several paths may lie ahead of you as they lead toward the range of options, and you can see where they begin to lead. Sometimes as you work on building the various paths, you find that several of the possibilities intersect with each other or inform each other. It is important to take the time to note these intersections and similarities. Do the crossing paths lead into a new option? If so, work on the new option too.

Sometimes the options just feel impossible, and the paths seem too long or difficult to achieve. Note your feelings on the sheet, and continue to work on the other options.

God's Open-Ended Options and Paths

As you work on developing and exploring the paths, you may come across one that feels as if it is from God, but stops abruptly because it's not possible to envision what comes next. The sudden stop may even come at the very beginning of the path. You find God calling you to an action, but you can't see the implications or ramifications of that action. This path may well be the one you are to follow (or it may not). If it is the path, God may be asking you to trust and step out faithfully with the understanding that God will open up the path in its own time. As you explore possible paths, take note of the one or ones where you feel God's presence most strongly.

Val illustrates a discernment challenge when the path she was following came to an abrupt end:

> I was in graduate school working toward a PhD in Old Testament in order to teach in a seminary. I had felt the call to teach more than five years earlier during my first year of seminary. I had worked three years as an associate pastor after seminary to gain experience in the church. When I left the pastorate to attend school, I knew I was following God's call. One Sunday on my way to church, I heard myself praying with words that seemed to come out of nowhere, "God, tell me what to do." I was so surprised at the prayer that I almost turned around and went home, but I headed on to church anyway. During worship I suddenly felt the Holy Spirit stirring inside of me and saying, "It's time to leave graduate school." I sat in the pew and just started crying and saying, "God, why are you calling me out of school?" What in the world would I do if I left school? I was surprised by the events of the morning, since my call to teach was strong.

> Now I felt God moving me in a different direction, and I had no idea what God could possibly be asking me to do next. I entered a process of discernment asking what God's longing for my life was. I kept coming up short. I heard the call to leave graduate school, but nothing was clear on the path after that action. I heard God saying, *I need you now, not after you finish school.* It finally became clear that God's desire was for me to leave school and then trust that God was working on "the rest of the story." I acted on God's call and withdrew from school without knowing what I was supposed to do other than trust.

> Ten months later I became the interim pastor of a church. It was a position that would eventually lead to my call to begin Water in the Desert Ministries. During the ten months while I waited for a ministry position, I found a job in a fast-food restaurant that paid my bills, taught me a lot, and used my ministry skills in new ways. I realized God's point was not the job I was

doing directly after leaving school, although God did not waste the time. God was calling me to leave school, nothing more and nothing less.

Many times we can't see the path ahead because the path is not ready, and God is working on other people who have to change in order for the path to open. Or perhaps we aren't ready to walk on this path. At these times, we must trust God to lead us into an uncertain future. At other times, the paths are relatively clear, and we follow them gladly.

The Path and Its Relationship with God

After filling out the sheets for each of the options and building the paths made up of the stepping-stones toward the options, step back for a bit and look at the various paths from a different perspective. Remember, spiritual discernment is about seeking God's desire for our lives. We need to examine each option and path from God's perspective.

Ask yourself questions that link you and God in each option. Does the path draw you nearer to God or move you farther away? Does the path keep you centered on Christ? Any choice you uncover should lead you into a deeper relationship with God. The path may lead you into an uncomfortable place, but the ultimate goal is to draw closer to God.

Where does each path take you as it relates to God?

Which ones seem to move you closer to God?

Which ones seem to take you farther away?

Fruits of the Spirit

Another way to explore whether or not each path leads closer to God is to look at Galatians 5:22-23, 25 and the fruits of the Spirit.

> The fruit of the Spirit is love, joy, peace, patience, kindness, generosity, faithfulness, gentleness, and self-control. There is no law against such things. . . . If we live by the Spirit, let us also be guided by the Spirit.

Using the text above, we need to ask questions like: *How does this path encourage fruits of the Spirit?* or *Does this path bring forth love or joy or peace or forgiveness?*

Return to each option and ask yourself whether the path leads toward any of the fruits of the Spirit.

For each option, write the fruits of the Spirit you see coming forth from that path.

If you don't see any fruits, make a note of that.

Dead-End Paths

You may come across paths that seem empty and don't lead anywhere or don't bring forth any fruits of the Spirit. If so, they are probably not the paths you need to walk down.

Do any of the paths, especially those that don't seem to bear any fruits of the Spirit, come to a dead end?

At this point you may have several paths ahead of you as you seek God's desire for your life. If one or more paths seem possible, move on to the next circle in the discernment diagram and go into the stage of *sifting* the possibilities.

It is possible at this point that none of the paths seems possible or draws you closer to God. If so, perhaps you've asked the wrong question, and you need to return to chapter 4 to re-address the issue and to re-form the questions—yet again.

CHAPTER 9

Sifting

YOU ARE FINALLY ready to sift all the data and allow a direction to emerge, pointing toward a decision and resolution of your issue. This circle involves a time of sorting, not additional data gathering. You are beginning to see which of the paths leads you closer to God. In order to choose one path over the others, you will sift the options and listen as you consider each possible path.

Two stories from Val's childhood may help to illustrate this part of the process of discernment:

> I remember helping my mother bake when I was growing up. The recipes usually called for a certain amount of sifted flour along with a few other ingredients like baking powder. I always wanted to measure the flour before I sifted it, but my mother kept telling me I didn't know how much flour I had until it was sifted (since the sifting added volume). I vividly remember putting wax paper on the counter, sifting flour onto the paper, and then carefully spooning the flour into the measuring cup. She always told me not to shake the flour because I would change the volume and therefore use too much flour.

> My father used to tell stories about his childhood in a small town. When he was growing up, the milk was delivered to the door every morning. The milk came straight from a dairy farm and was not processed like our milk today. My dad and his siblings would race down to the kitchen in the mornings, because the first one there could eat the cream that had risen to the top of the bottle.

Neither of these experiences is common today because flour is presifted and milk is processed, but they remind us of earlier practices. The flour example

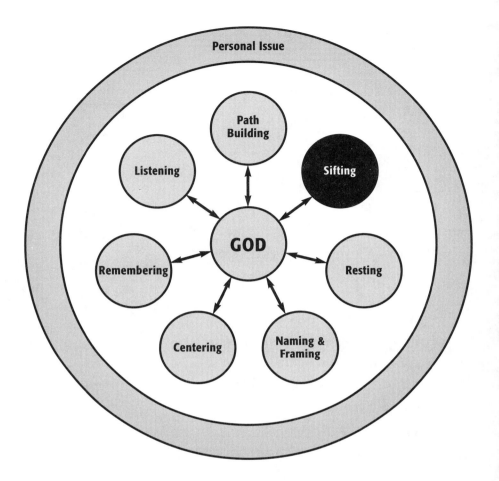

reminds us that until we take time to sift, we don't know what we have. In the other story, we have a wonderful vision of the best part rising to the top. It may be in our world we have lost the willingness to "sift" because we no longer see its value. We lack hands-on experience that demonstrates the importance of sifting to the whole process.

Which Path Emerges Most Clearly?

In some respects the sifting circle of discernment involves waiting. It is a time to step back and look at the whole picture in an inactive way. It is a time to let go of control and see what rises to the top. At this stage in our movement toward making a decision, we are passive and allow God to be the actor or leader. We ask only one central question in this circle: *Which path emerges most clearly?* In other words, on which path does the Spirit rest? The right path may not rise up immediately. You may need to give it some time.

Letting go of control is scary. Take a minute to think about trust, because for sifting to work, we need to:

- trust the Holy Spirit to be involved
- trust the process to bring forth insight
- trust that God wants abundance for you
- trust that God's yearning tends toward wholeness—shalom.

Such a level of trust asks that we let go of our need to be in control. The ability to trust in God alone, to trust that God will provide good for us, calls us to have a faith deeply centered in experiences of God's trustworthiness.

List areas where you have a hard time trusting the Holy Spirit and the abundance God wants for you.

If you are struggling with trust, return to chapter 2 and review the section on images for God. What images are helpful at this stage?

Pray the following prayer:

Loving God who created me, remind me that you want the best for my life. Help me trust that the Holy Spirit is involved in this process and that I do not have to do it all. Give me courage to let go of the control and realize the possibilities for transformation and new life awaiting me. In the name of the One who walks with me, Jesus the Christ, Amen.

Read over the information you have gathered about all the paths. Which one stirs positive emotions in you? Right now focus on looking for the path that brings you closer to God.

Do the following exercise in your journal or just by closing your eyes:

In your mind, allow yourself to walk the path or paths that seem most promising. Among the paths that lead you closer to God, continue to listen as you imagine each one. Let the scene change moment by moment. Allow Jesus to walk a path with you to see how it feels. If the path you felt was the best doesn't continue to feel right, allow God to redirect your thoughts to another possible path.

Now that you have walked the paths in prayer, it is time to ask yourself some questions regarding the specific path you have chosen.

Write down the path that has risen to the surface. Where do you see it leading you?

Can you feel the Spirit resting on this path?

Do you see any fruits of the Spirit arise on this path? (See chapter 8.)

What changes would you make to the path?

Do the changes allow the Holy Spirit to remain with you on the path?

You may very well alter this path somewhat in time, and aspects may change as you gain understanding or events affect living it out. Keep in mind two points from chapter 1: we will not have 100 percent clarity, and God asks us to be honest and to walk faithfully. You may also feel God's yearning could lead you down more than one path, and that is okay. Because we are human beings and have free will, God's yearning for our lives is multifaceted.

Consolation or Desolation? (or Confusion in the Middle)

Now that you have chosen one path to follow toward resolution of your issue, one more step remains. You are confident God calls you to this path at this time. Let the decision simmer for a bit, and then ask yourself how you are feeling about the decision.

Ignatius of Loyola describes this feeling as either *consolation* or *desolation*. This interior movement and response comes at the end of the complex process in which you have examined the issue, worked on decision making, sorted the data, and identified the paths. Now ask, *Does the path that is rising to the level of affirmation bring consolation (a sense of moving closer to God) or desolation (a sense of being separated from God)?* In other words, if the decision is of God, your heart will be consoled with feelings of joy, tranquility, peace, and trust. If the decision is not of God, you will feel uneasy or sense a heaviness in your heart or a weight on your shoulders. And there is a third option: confusion in the middle, where neither complete consolation nor complete desolation prevails.

If the path that has risen to the surface brings consolation, you can go on to identify what feels good about it. The path beckoning you may be a difficult one. Once again you may need to address fears that this path elicits. Perhaps you need to hear the angels saying "Be not afraid," imparting courage to face a path full of God's yearning and abundance but possibly also intimidating or frightening.

Does the path you are considering bring you consolation?

Does it bring you closer to who God is calling you to be?

What feels good about it?

Where are your fears? Where do you need to hear the angels say "Do not be afraid"?

On the other hand, if the path is bringing desolation, ask what feels uncomfortable about it and why? Is the desolation due to fear? If so, examine the fear. Is the fear due to the unknown, or is God asking you to do something you have thought you would never do? If the answer to the latter question is yes, your decision may be right; return to chapter 5 and reread the section on holy indifference.

However, if you sense fear because the decision is actually dangerous or unsafe, then determine what feels unsafe about it. You may very well say, *It just doesn't feel right*. Listen to that intuition. Sometimes fears are appropriate and keep us from venturing into danger. Listen carefully to sort the voices and their messages.

You may need to revisit the possible paths and look them over again. Once more allow God into the process, and ask which path God wishes for you to travel. Ask yourself these questions.

Is the path I am considering bringing desolation?

Is it drawing me farther from God?

What feels uncomfortable about it?

Is the desolation due to fear; if so, what is causing the fear?

If you find yourself confused, answering "both" to the question *Does it bring consolation or desolation?* perhaps you have not seen an aspect to this path or have not yet let go of a blockage standing in the way. Confusion at this stage indicates that you have overlooked a dimension or possibility. Review the process to discover what you have forgotten, missed, or not let go of; then look at your options again.

More Considerations

Even when we are feeling consolation about a path, we need to examine closely the reasons for our consolation. Gordon Smith raises an important issue regarding consolation. We need to ask ourselves once again what our motives are. We need to test the consolation to see whether it makes us comfortable but is not God's desire. Or is the peace from God?[1]

The questions in the next section will help you examine the feelings from another angle. If these questions raise uncertainty about the consolation you are feeling, return to chapter 4 and review the issue you have identified and the questions. You may need to refine the question you are asking or consider whether you have listened to all the voices (see chapter 7). Repeating the process will bring you closer to God's yearning for your life.

Some Questions to Ask Yourself

1. Does this path make me feel good because it rights a wrong experienced earlier in my life? Example: *I was told as a child that I wasn't important, and this will make me feel important; therefore I have peace about it.*

2. Does this path make me feel good because I will look good to my family and colleagues? *Return to the fruits of the Spirit (chapter 8). Does this decision make you feel good because it brings forth a fruit of the Spirit and also brings you closer to God?*

3. Does the decision or path draw me closer to God? *This question pinpoints your consolation/confusion/desolation. Take time to process your fears and make sure they are not getting in the way of seeing whether the path draws you closer to God.*

4. Am I being asked to leave something I love, to move into something unknown?

5. Is God stretching me? How?

A path has risen clearly, and now you have lifted it up to God in prayer. You have begun to determine whether this path or decision rests well in your soul. The next chapter will take you into a period of resting.

CHAPTER 10

Resting

SO OFTEN in our lives we make decisions and
then jump right into the activities required to bring
the decisions to fruition. Society teaches us to take
action: make a decision and then act on it. Spiritual
discernment teaches us to wait before acting. The
discernment process prescribes rest at this stage.

We need to live with the results of our discernment process for a while. As we live with what we
have discovered, we will review our issue, the ques-
tions, the holy indifference, and the letting go of our values so we may hear
God's values. Through all these stages, we experience a growth in feeling and
in faith. If we are busy acting rather than waiting, we may miss something—
an observation, an insight, a slight turning of direction from God. So often
someone says, "I thought I made the right decision, but nothing worked." The
problems usually come because the person jumped into action too soon before
realizing that the path was not within God's yearning for him or her.

Sabbath and Rest

In his book *Sabbath: Finding Rest, Renewal, and Delight in Our Busy Lives,*
Wayne Muller describes the rhythm of sabbath time. He reflects on our busy
lives that move from activity to activity without sufficient space or time to rest.
The commandment regarding the sabbath gives us permission, and indeed
helps us to see the necessity, to stop and learn to become reflective. The fourth
commandment says:

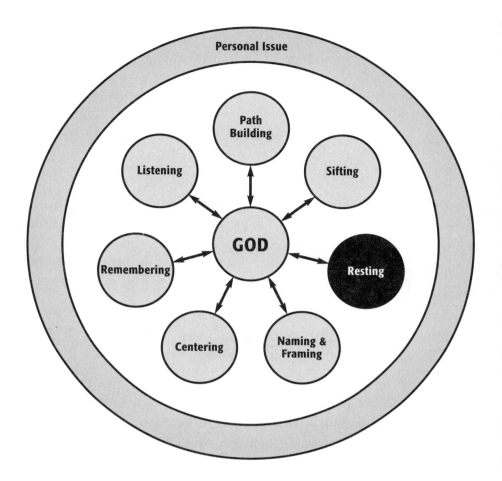

Observe [remember] the sabbath day and keep it holy, as the LORD, your God commanded you. Six days you shall labor and do all your work. But the seventh day is a sabbath to the LORD your God; you shall not do any work— you, or your son or your daughter, or your male or female slave, or your ox or your donkey, or any of your livestock, or the resident alien in your towns, so that your male and female slave may rest as well as you.
—DEUTERONOMY 5:12-14

Deuteronomy 5 traces the origin of the sabbath day to the Hebrews' deliverance from slavery in Egypt; the Lord God brought them out and commanded observance of the sabbath day. In Exodus 20 the sabbath is related to God's acts of creation: the Lord rested on the seventh day and therefore blessed it and made it holy (Gen. 2:1-3).

Today, we find ourselves caught up in a cycle of busyness. Our lives are full of appointments, work, and activities. Being busy may impart a sense of accomplishment and fulfillment. Or we may feel tired from all our busyness. Or perhaps we don't exactly know what to feel. At least we know we are actively trying to keep up with the tasks in front of us. "But Sabbath says, Be still. Stop. There is no rush to get to the end, because we are never finished. Take time to rest, and eat, and drink, and be refreshed. And in the gentle rhythm of that refreshment, listen to the sound the heart makes as it speaks the quiet truth of what is needed."[1] Part of learning the process of discernment involves recovering the rhythm of sabbath rest.

This final circle, focused on resting, calls us to enter a sabbath period in which the information gathered in the previous circles sinks into our understanding and becomes clear. Remember the illustration from the Tao Te Ching: *Who is it that can make muddy water clear? But if allowed to remain still, it will gradually become clear of itself.*[2] The sabbath rhythm provides the paradigm for rest and clarification in the midst of our actions and our activity.

We can also look to scripture to appreciate the importance of this sabbath rhythm. Particularly in the Gospel of Luke, Jesus' balanced pattern of involvement in people's lives alternating with retreat from activity to rest and pray instructs us. This rhythm punctuates Luke's story. Beginning in Luke 3:21, at his baptism, Jesus prays and receives the Holy Spirit. After his time in the wilderness, the temptations, and his first healing experiences, Jesus retreats to a deserted place to rest (4:42). The rhythm becomes clear after Jesus calls his first disciples and continues teaching and healing. Jesus would withdraw to deserted places and pray (5:16). Prior to the major decision regarding which disciples to name as the Twelve, Jesus goes out to the mountain and spends the night in prayer (6:12). Then, together they go to a level place, and Jesus delivers his Sermon on the Plain (6:17-49). The combination of active ministry and withdrawing from the crowds to spend time in prayer continues throughout Jesus' ministry. He includes the disciples (9:28) and responds to their yearning for being taught how to pray (11:1-2). The rhythm of withdrawing, gaining perspective, and being able to listen through communication with God enables us to learn the rhythm of discipleship.

The same pattern appears in the story of Creation in Genesis 1. God actively creates and then stands back to reflect upon what has been done and calls it "good" (Gen. 1:4, 10, 12, 18, 21, 25, 31). Becoming attuned to the rhythm of creation, to the flow of the seasons of the year, and even to the shifts of day into night all become the framework for the ways we can learn to be active and to rest. In sabbath rest, we are following the commandment and the model of our God who rested on the seventh day and was refreshed (Exod. 31:17).

Remembering the Process

Even though you have done a lot of writing and reflecting throughout this process, we are going to ask you to write and reflect one more time. In this final stage, reflect on the entire process, allowing the feelings of consolation or desolation to sink in at a deeper level.

Spend some time reflecting on what you have done throughout this discernment process. Summarize what you have learned and felt and the actions you have taken. You may want to read through what you have written in this workbook to facilitate your reflection. Then ask yourself the following questions.

After remembering the process, how do I feel about it?

What new observations or insights arose as I reviewed the whole experience?

Do I continue to feel consolation or desolation, or have the feelings changed?

Prayer

Another aspect of resting is prayer. You have remembered your discernment process and acknowledged your conclusion. At this stage your ongoing prayer involves two components: lifting up and letting go. Your hard work in the discernment process has brought you to a point where you feel you have discerned God's desire for this time and place in your life. Lift up to God in prayer the path that lies before you. You can give the decision to God and ask for further guidance and continued leading. In this way you will enter into holy indifference at a deeper level and let go of the outcome. As you do so, rest in the Spirit, listen to God, and continue to notice how you are feeling about the decision.

Here are two prayers that might be fruitful at this juncture. As you pray either or both prayers, try opening your hands—even raising them toward God—as a physical expression of releasing the decision to God.

> Loving God, who created all things and who is full of grace, you have sent your Son and Spirit to walk with me through this process of discernment. Thank you for your guidance and the courage to face the issue that has been before me. I lift my decision _____ (describe the decision) up to you. It seems to me that it is the yearning you have for my life at this time. I let it go and give it back to you so that I may rest in your Spirit. If it is not from you, give me eyes to see and ears to hear what you would have me do next. If it is from you, take it, transform it; and if it is your yearning, let it come back to me with love and grace. Open the path before me that I may walk this journey and continue to listen to your longing for my life. Give me courage and strength to move forward. Eternal God, we see through a glass dimly, so there is uncertainty in my heart about whether I have made the right decision. Help my uncertainty. Remind me that you have asked me to be faithful. In the name of the One who taught us to pray, "Thy will be done," Jesus Christ my Lord and Savior. Amen.

The second prayer comes from Flora Wuellner. She calls this prayer the "radical prayer" and uses it whenever she is in a discernment process about something new emerging in her life.

> God, if this new activity . . . relationship . . . interest . . . personality change . . . is right for me, let it take root and increase in my life. If it is wrong for me, let it become less and less important to me, and let it decrease in my life.[3]

"Do not be conformed to this world, but be transformed by the renewing of your minds, so that you may discern what is the will of God—what is good and acceptable and perfect."

—Romans 12:2

Waiting to Share

We need to rest with our decision about the path chosen for a while before sharing our decision with others. In this way we allow God to speak to our heart first. If we speak too soon, others' reactions to our decision may speak louder than God's voice. Sometimes people around us are not listening to God's desire and cannot discern for us, so they may not honor God's yearning for us. We need to rest with God before other voices become too strong.

We also need to give ourselves time to reach a level of comfort with the change. Holding the decision lightly allows it to soak in. Remember opening your hands to release the path and the decision into God's keeping. When we have our fists wrapped tightly around the decision, we cannot relax, and we are holding it rather than God.

It is possible, as we wait, that we will realize this decision is not the one God would have us make. If this happens, we just need to move back to the possible paths and look them over again. Or maybe we need to reexamine our fears. In some cases it will be best to return to the framed question and see if it needs to be shifted.

When you see God's light shining on a path, when it brings consolation, you have found the best possible option for this time in your life. Congratulations! You have walked through a long and difficult process. Take a deep breath and relax. Give thanks to God for the guidance of the Holy Spirit and the example of those who have gone before us. Now you may begin living into the answers.

Concluding and Beginning

You have reached the end of the discernment process. You have asked God a question regarding an issue in your life. You have walked a path of discernment. Now you are ready to face the future our loving God yearns for you to live. Once you've decided on a path and begin following it, you will need to continue the discernment process. You will face smaller decisions along the way. For instance, God may ask you to change jobs and move; once you are in the new city, you must decide where to live. God may call you to start a business, and you must decide where God is leading you in developing the business.

So you still have a lot of work to do as you live into the future. You may have doubts and fears; continue to lift them up to God and have courage. God will not abandon you. Remember, even though you have made the decision, God may still be putting things into place. Be patient and don't rush what can't be rushed.

Discernment is an art, so the more you practice, the easier it will become. With large issues or small decisions, God continually supports and encourages naming, centering, remembering, listening, path building, sifting, and resting processes. With the grace of God you will eventually find that discernment becomes a way of life.

NOTES

INTRODUCTION

1. Thomas Green, *Weeds Among the Wheat: Discernment: Where Prayer and Action Meet* (Notre Dame: Ave Maria Press, 1984), 11.

CHAPTER 1

1. Chuck Olsen, *Transforming Church Boards into Communities of Spiritual Leaders* (Bethesda, MD: Alban Institute, 1995), 86.

2. Pierre Wolff, *Discernment: The Art of Choosing Well*, rev. ed. (Liguori, MO: Liguori/Triumph Books, 200), 12–13.

3. Gordon T. Smith, *Listening to God in Times of Choice: The Art of Discerning God's Will* (Downers Grove, IL: InterVarsity Press, 1997), 28.

4. Wayne Muller, *Sabbath: Finding Rest, Renewal, and Delight in Our Busy Lives*. New York: Bantam Books, 2000 26, 1.

5. Smith, *Listening to God*, 65.

6. Green, *Weeds Among the Wheat*, 67.

CHAPTER 2

1. David Keirsey and Marilyn Bates, *Please Understand Me: Character and Temperament Types* (Del Mar, CA: Prometheus Nemesis Book Company, 1984), 5–10.

2. Wilke W. and Noreen Cannon Au, *The Discerning Heart: Exploring the Christian Path* (New York: Paulist Press, 2006), 104–06.

3. Danny E. Morris and Charles M. Olsen, *Discerning God's Will Together: A Spiritual Practice for the Church* (Bethesda, MD: Alban Institute, 1997), 36.

4. Wendy M. Wright, "Passing Angels: The Arts of Spiritual Discernment," in *Weavings* 10, no. 6 (November/December 1995):10-11.

CHAPTER 3

1. Green, *Weeds Among the Wheat*, 64.

2. Dallas Willard, *The Spirit of the Disciplines: Understanding How God Changes Lives* (San Francisco: HarperSanFrancisco, 1991), ix.

3. Richard Foster, *Celebration of Discipline: The Path to Spiritual Growth*, Rev. ed. (San Francisco: HarperSanFrancisco, 1988), 2.

4. Jane Vennard, *A Praying Congregation: The Art of Teaching Spiritual Practice* (Herndon, VA: Alban Institute, 2005), 75.

5. John Ackerman, *Spiritual Awakening: A Guide to Spiritual Life in Congregations* (Bethesda, MD: Alban Institute, 1994), 21.

6. Thomas Browne, quoted in Madeleine L'Engle, *A Ring of Endless Light* (New York: Dell Publishing Co., 1980), 24.

CHAPTER 5

1. Richard M. Gula, *Moral Discernment* (New York: Paulist Press, 1997), 57.

2. Au and Au, *The Discerning Heart*, 60.

3. Morris and Olsen, *Discerning God's Will Together*, 74.

CHAPTER 5

1. Maureen Conroy, *The Discerning Heart: Discovering a Personal God* (Chicago: Loyola University Press, 1993),15.

CHAPTER 9

1. Smith, *Listening to God in Times of Choice*, 56–65.

CHAPTER 10

1. Wayne Muller, *Sabbath: Finding Rest, Renewal, and Delight in Our Busy Lives* (New York: Bantam Books, 2000), 85.

2. Ibid., 26.

3. Flora Wuellner, "Were Not Our Hearts Burning Within Us?" *Weavings* 10, no. 6 (November/December 1995):31.

BIBLIOGRAPHY

Ackerman, John. *Spiritual Awakening: A Guide to Spiritual Life in Congregations.* Bethesda, MD: Alban Institute, 1994.

Au, Wilkie, and Noreen Cannon Au. *The Discerning Heart: Exploring the Christian Path.* New York: Paulist Press, 2006.

Blythe, Teresa A. *50 Ways to Pray: Practices from Many Traditions and Times.* Nashville: Abingdon Press, 2006.

Conroy, Maureen. *The Discerning Heart: Discovering a Personal God.* Chicago: Loyola University Press, 1993.

Consultation on Common Texts, The. *The Revised Common Lectionary.* Nashville: Abingdon Press, 1992.

Dunnam, Maxie. *The Workbook on Spiritual Disciplines.* Nashville: Upper Room Books, 1984.

Foster, Richard J. *Celebration of Discipline: The Path to Spiritual Growth.* Rev. ed. San Francisco: HarperSanFrancisco, 1988.

Green, Thomas H. *Weeds among the Wheat: Discernment: Where Prayer and Action Meet.* Notre Dame: Ave Maria Press, 1984.

Gula, Richard M. *Moral Discernment.* New York: Paulist Press, 1997.

Job, Rueben P., comp. *A Guide to Spiritual Discernment.* Nashville: Upper Room Books, 1996.

Jones, L. Gregory. *Embodying Forgiveness: A Theological Analysis.* Grand Rapids, MI: Wm. B. Eerdmans Publishing Company, 1995.

Keirsey, David, and Marilyn Bates. *Please Understand Me: Character and Temperament Types.* Del Mar, CA: Prometheus Nemesis Book Co., 1984.

L'Engle, Madeleine. *A Ring of Endless Light.* New York: Dell Publishing Co., 1980.

Metz, Barbara, and John Burchill. *The Enneagram and Prayer: Discovering Our True Selves Before God.* Denville, NJ: Dimension Books, 1987.

Michael, Chester P., and Marie C. Norrisey. *Prayer and Temperament: Different Prayer Forms for Different Personality Types.* Charlottesville, VA: Open Door, 1984.

Morris, Danny E., and Charles M. Olsen. *Discerning God's Will Together: A Spiritual Practice for the Church.* Bethesda, MD: Alban Institute, 1997.

Morseth, Ellen. *Ritual and the Arts in Spiritual Discernment.* Kansas City, MO: Worshipful-Work: Centering for Transforming Religious Leadership, 1999.

Muller, Wayne. *Sabbath: Finding Rest, Renewal, and Delight in Our Busy Lives.* New York: Bantam Books, 2000.

Olsen, Charles M. *Transforming Church Boards into Communities of Spiritual Leaders.* Bethesda, MD: Alban Institute, 1995.

Riso, Don Richard, and Russ Hudson. *The Wisdom of the Enneagram: The Complete Guide to Psychological and Spiritual Growth for the Nine Personality Types.* New York: Bantam Books, 1999.

Smith, Gordon T. *Listening to God in Times of Choice: The Art of Discerning God's Will.* Downers Grove, IL: InterVarsity Press, 1997.

Vennard, Jane E. *A Praying Congregation: The Art of Teaching Spiritual Practice.* Herndon, VA: Alban Institute, 2005.

Via, Dan O., Jr. *Self-Deception and Wholeness in Paul and Matthew.* Minneapolis, MN: Augsburg Fortress, 1990.

Warren, Rick. *Personal Bible Study Methods to Study the Bible on Your Own.* Grand Rapids, MI: Zondervan, 2005.

Willard, Dallas. *The Spirit of the Disciplines: Understanding How God Changes Lives.* San Francisco: HarperSanFrancisco, 1991.

Wolff, Pierre. *Discernment: The Art of Choosing Well.* Rev. ed. Liguori, MO: Liguori/Triumph Books, 2003.

Wolpert, Daniel. *Creating a Life with God: The Call of Ancient Prayer Practices.* Nashville, Tenn.: Upper Room Books, 2003.

Wright, Wendy M. "Passing Angels: The Arts of Spiritual Discernment." *Weavings: A Journal of the Christian Life.* 10, no. 6 (Nov./Dec. 1995):6–15. Issue theme is "Discerning the Spirits."

Wuellner, Flora. "Were Not Our Hearts Burning Within Us?" in *Weavings: A*

Journal of the Christian Life. 10, no. 6, (Nov./Dec. 1995):27-36. Issue theme is "Discerning the Spirits."

Web sites:

Alban Institute: www.alban.org
Enneagram self test: www.enneagraminstitute.com
Myers-Briggs: www.personalitypathways.com/type_inventory.html
V. Isenhower Photography: www.visenhowerphotography.com

Water in the Desert Ministries

www.waterinthedesert.org

ABOUT THE AUTHORS

VALERIE K. ISENHOWER is executive director of Water in the Desert Ministries and owner of V. Isenhower Photography. She received her undergraduate education at University of Montana and University of Northern Colorado. She earned an MDiv from Central Baptist Theological Seminary in Kansas City and pursued additional graduate work at Graduate Theological Union in Berkeley, California. As a photographer, Val specializes in meditative and discernment photographs. She also takes hot-air-balloon photos. Her photographs have been published and displayed in galleries.

JUDITH A. TODD is program director for Water in the Desert Ministries. She received her undergraduate education from Hastings College and University of New Mexico. She earned an MDiv from McCormick Theological Seminary, an MA in Hebrew Bible and a PhD in Biblical Studies from Graduate Theological Union in Berkeley, California. A former seminary lecturer and associate professor, she now also leads retreats in spiritual formation and biblical interpretation.

journal

journal

journal

journal

journal